STAR WARS
Vs.
STAR TREK

Forewords by
JEREMY BULLOCH (Boba Fett in Star Wars)
and TIM RUSS (Tuvok in *Star Trek: Voyager*)

STAR WARS

vs.

STAR TREK

COULD THE EMPIRE KICK THE FEDERATION'S ASS?
and other galaxy-shaking enigmas

Matt Forbeck

Avon, Massachusetts

Published by
Adams Media, a division of F+W Media, Inc.
57 Littlefield Street, Avon, MA 02322. U.S.A.
www.adamsmedia.com

ISBN 10: 1-4405-1262-0
ISBN 13: 978-1-4405-1262-9
eISBN 10: 1-4405-2576-5
eISBN 13: 978-1-4405-2576-6

Printed in the United States of America.

10 9 8 7 6 5 4 3 2 1

Library of Congress Cataloging-in-Publication Data
is available from the publisher.

This book is available at quantity discounts for bulk purchases.
For information, please call 1-800-289-0963.

Contents

PART I: People

PART II: Gadgets

PART III: Time and Space

ACKNOWLEDGMENTS

Thanks to Peter Archer for approaching me about this book and encouraging me to write it. And thanks to Phil Athans for helping make it read so well.

Thanks also to Lisa Stevens, Jeremy Bulloch, Sara Char, Tim Russ, Mike Stackpole, and Ken Hite for their generous contributions.

Special thanks to George Lucas and Gene Roddenberry for creating Star Wars and Star Trek, firing the imaginations of generations of kids and adults.

Finally, thanks to my wife, Ann, and my kids, Marty, Pat, Ken, Nick, and Helen, for supporting me through all of my projects and everything else I do.

FOREWORD

Jeremy Bulloch (Boba Fett)

Star Wars or Star Trek? It's a question I get asked all the time. I have been a fan of Star Trek since the original series, when I loved watching great characters such as Captain Kirk, Spock, Scotty, and Bones. Many years later I saw the film *Star Wars: A New Hope*, and no one can ever forget the opening titles with the Imperial spaceship roaring above your head. This was a major piece of cinema history. In movie theatres around the world there were audible cries of *Awesome! Wow!* and *Cool!* I knew then that Star Wars was going to be very, very special.

Little did I know that I would be lucky enough to work on Episode II—er . . . I think I mean Episode V, playing the small part of Boba Fett in *The Empire Strikes Back*, followed later by a reprise of my role in *Return of the Jedi*. Being involved with the Star Wars project was, and still is, one of the highlights of my career.

There is no doubt that Star Wars has a larger following, with fans from two to eighty-two years old. It is incredible to think that, after more than thirty years, Star Wars is still as popular as it was on its release in 1977. Not a day goes by without my being reminded of Star Wars and the fact that I played Boba Fett. (I must stop wearing that bucket on my head!)

I suppose I should be biased when it comes to citing a preference between Star Wars and Star Trek. But I find it difficult to make a clear choice between the two. Despite belonging to the same genre, they are also very different, retain their own merits, and have their own following of fans. No convention would be the same without an appearance from the outrageous "Klingons," for example. Overall, however, I think that Star Wars just gets the nod over Star Trek, particularly for its special effects and music.

I have had the pleasure of meeting many of the Star Trek cast at various conventions around the world. One of my favorite actors from the Next Generation series is Marina Sirtis, who played the bridge officer Deanna Troi. Not only is she a very talented actress, but also she is smart enough to support the same soccer team as I do in England. Every time we meet up at an event we have a long conversation about the fortunes of our club, Tottenham Hotspur.

The Star Wars Vs. Star Trek argument is one that could go on and on indefinitely, and by coming down on the side of Star Wars, I probably risk having my jetpack bashed up by some serious Star Trek fan. Let's not forget, however, that it's all fiction and there to be enjoyed. "Beam me up, Scotty" and "May the Force be with you all!"

—Jeremy Bulloch

FOREWORD

Tim Russ (Tuvok)

It is difficult to find common elements in Star Trek and Star Wars to serve as a basis of comparison as to which concept is better. Star Trek began and has continued primarily as a television series. Feature films were produced afterward. In contrast, Star Wars began as a series of feature films.

The original Star Wars feature films were one story presented in a three-film arc, told in about six hours. Star Trek, a long-running TV series, was composed of many different and, for the most part, standalone stories.

Given that difference in the way the two concepts have been presented, the playing field is uneven right off the bat. The creators and writers of Star Trek had the very difficult task of putting together a unique cast of characters that had to draw the audience into their various relationships and trials every week over a very long period of time. The task of the feature writers for Star Wars, on the other hand, was to tell a story in a very short period of time, although they still had to bring together an interesting cast of characters to enact that story.

The best way to compare the two series is to find the common ground they share.

Both concepts, I think, include very interesting and unique characters that take the viewer through the stories and keep the audience engaged.

Both shows are part of the science fiction genre. As far as that goes, both demonstrate miles of sci-fi technology, alien characters, and unknown phenomena.

But as to themes, I do think there is a difference between the two. Star Wars is a classic medieval theme dressed up as an action-adventure. David fights Goliath, rebels battle against the Empire, and throughout runs the Greek tragic theme of the son in conflict with the father and the inner turmoil that creates on both sides. Star Wars also taps in to the Eastern philosophy of inner strength, the mind and body as one. And although there are human characters and attributes, Star Wars does not take place anywhere near Earth—in fact, it's not even in our galaxy. Nothing you see in the Star Wars trilogies is related to Earth's human history. The Star Wars world is self-contained.

Star Trek, on the other hand, originates on Earth and takes place in our solar system and galaxy. We, as the audience, can relate to the familiar images, concepts, and ideas that are laced throughout the Trek stories, as the series takes the human experience, past and present, and projects it into the future. Since its first incarnation, the Star Trek series has used interaction with aliens and the exploration of the unknown to play out the social struggles, differences, and norms of our human society. We can see and examine ourselves through the actions of the heroes as they confront unique circumstances and make difficult decisions (or misinterpretations) while trying to solve, question, or on occasion do battle with other alien beings and their societies.

By watching these stories unfold, we can, in fact, learn about ourselves. In the Trek world, wealth and power do not rule the day. There is a sense of equality and a level playing field. There is no outright discrimination against those who may be different than others. Judgment and opinion is based on character, which I think is one of Star Trek's most endearing qualities.

Though both the Star Wars and Star Trek franchises have been immensely successful and enjoyed by millions, I think Star Trek edges out Star Wars as the better of the two, only because of its relationship to Earth's human history and experience.

But then, I'm a bit biased.

—Tim Russ

Introduction

Since the summer afternoon in June 1977 when the first Trekkie wandered out of the theater after seeing *Star Wars: A New Hope* and wondered aloud what all the fuss was about, fans of Star Wars and fans of Star Trek have been butting heads with each other.

The difference between Star Wars fans and Trekkies is as stark as night and day. Star Wars fans prefer a story that started "a long time ago in a galaxy far, far away." They don't care about *how* a lightsaber works, they just love the cool *pkshhhhhhh!* sound it makes when it clashes against another one. They couldn't give a damn that a parsec is a unit of distance, not time. The universe doesn't have to make sense, as long as it feels right.

Trekkies, on the other hand, like their stories to be about science and exploration in a hopeful future. Their hearts beat faster when Data starts reconfiguring the main sensor array to emit a focused beam of chronotons. They love watching Scotty rig an array of photon torpedoes to cause an atmospheric inversion that will prevent a planet from imploding.

Beyond that, the basic difference between the two franchises comes down to a pair of four-letter words.

Star Trek is about a *trek*, a journey, a series of missions that bring humanity farther out into the galaxy so that we can learn more about ourselves. It's about exploring, learning, and discovering new things: "To boldly go where no one has gone before."

Star Wars, on the other hand, is about *wars*, conflict, and the battle between good and evil that's fought not only on the battlefield but within our own souls. Star Wars is about seeking adventure, uncovering secret plans, rescuing princesses: "Restoring freedom to the galaxy."

Which side you take up in this decades-old argument between two of the most popular entertainment sagas of all time depends on which of those two sets of ideas mean the most to you.

But wait! We can't just let it go with that. No way! Would Captain Kirk walk away from a bar fight with a Klingon? Hah! Would Han Solo miss the chance to grab some glory for himself? I don't think so! We have a chance to pit the heroes, villains, ships, weapons, and themes of these two franchises against each other in head-to-head battle. And we're going to do it.

Will this settle the argument about which saga is best for all time? Of course not. The hottest lightsaber couldn't slice through that Gordian (La Forge) Knot. But it's going to be fun to try!

PART 1

PEOPLE

Throughout this book, you'll find a series of multiple choice quizzes designed to help you figure out which sci-fi saga you care more about. Keep a running tally at the end of each chapter. When you get to the end of the book, you can add up all your scores and see where you fall.

Then start arguing about whether or not you agree with the results.

1. **Han Solo was frozen in:**
   A. Liquid nitrogen C. Carbonite
   B. Solid steel D. Margaritaville

2. **Captain Benjamin Sisko's favorite sport is:**
   A. Fencing C. Cricket
   B. Baseball D. Soccer

3. **Sir Alec Guinness (the elder Obi-Wan Kenobi) won an Academy Award for his role in:**
   A. *The Bridge on the River Kwai*
   B. *Star Wars: A New Hope*
   C. *Smiley's People*
   D. *Lawrence of Arabia*

4. **In *Star Trek: The Original Series*, Captain James T. Kirk was born in Iowa. In *Star Trek (2009)*, he was born:**
   A. In Wisconsin
   B. In San Francisco
   C. Aboard the USS *Kelvin*
   D. Aboard the *Enterprise (NX-01)*

5. **Luke Skywalker's Uncle Owen and Aunt Beru farm:**
   A. Corn C. Sandworms
   B. Silicate D. Moisture

6. **The first captain of the *Enterprise* NCC-1701 was:**
   A. James Kirk C. Christopher Pyke
   B. Jonathan Archer D. Gates McFadden

Answers: 1. C, 2. B, 3. A, 4. C, 5. D, 6. C

CHAPTER 1

MEN
Masters of the Universe

The men of Star Wars and Star Trek form the bulk of the heroes of both series. That's partly because each series was created in the sixties and seventies, back when the women's rights movement was just cresting, and part of it is due to the fact that the vast majority of people who consume science fiction—whether in film, book, comic, or game form—are young men. While more women and girls devour science fiction today than ever before, it's still a field that boys and men dominate.

Despite that, both Star Wars and Star Trek did a lot to step outside of what their original audiences expected from them. Setting stories in a distant future (or a long time ago in a galaxy far, far away) forces a narrative distance between the viewer and the story. Filling that distance with fictional years allows viewers to be a lot more open-minded and forgiving about strange new things (planets, civilizations, girls) than they might otherwise tolerate. That's why the first inter-racial kiss ever shown on a U.S. television drama appeared on an episode of *Star Trek*—between Captain Kirk and Lieutenant Uhura. Even then, though, the two of them had to be telekinetically forced into locking lips.

The guys of Star Wars run the gamut from swashbuckling pulp heroes to yearning farm boys to wise teachers. The men of Star Trek, on the other hand, tend to be a bit more reserved, scholars rather than scoundrels, people sent out to explore the galaxy, not exploit it.

To figure out which of these people are the best at what they do, we're going to pluck pairs of them from specific points in their times and pit them against each other.

THE WISE OLD MEN

With age comes wisdom, or so we should all be fortunate enough to discover if we're lucky enough to live that long. Before the older men take their final voyage to the Undiscovered Country, they hope to bequeath a bit of knowledge to the heroes slated to take their places. Let's take a couple of these wise men and pit them against each other to see how well they manage.

BEN KENOBI VS. CAPTAIN PICARD

BEN KENOBI

OCCUPATION: Crazy old wizard

DATAPOINT: Actor Alec Guiness (Obi-Wan Kenobi) celebrated his sixty-second birthday while filming *Star Wars: A New Hope* in Tunisia/Tatooine.

SNAPSHOT: Obi-Wan Kenobi, as he was once known, has been hiding out on Tatooine for the past nineteen years, watching over Luke Skywalker from a distance. He's led a solitary life, keeping himself and Luke secret from the Empire for that entire time. He appears to have succeeded, despite the fact that placing Darth Vader's infant son with Vader's own half-brother might have seemed a too-obvious hiding place. Kenobi's ward doesn't know him well at all, but Obi-Wan believes the boy will come through for him in the end. He holds on to that belief because he doesn't have much else left.

CAPTAIN JEAN-LUC PICARD

OCCUPATION: Starship captain

DATAPOINT: Actor Patrick Stewart (Captain Picard) was forty-seven when he took command of the *Enterprise* in the *Star Trek: The Next Generation* pilot episode "Encounter at Farpoint."

SNAPSHOT: When Picard assumes command of the starship designated *NCC-1701-D*, he takes on a new challenge with a fresh crew in the latest model of the *Enterprise,* the previous versions of which were all destroyed. Despite that unfortunate streak and his untested crew running a ship filled with 1,014 souls—including hundreds of civilians—Picard seems confident in his ability to mold his officers into the finest bridge crew in Starfleet. His primary protégé is Commander Will Riker, a career officer who serves as his second-in-command.

WHO'D WIN?

Kenobi enters Ten Forward, the first known bar on any of Star Trek's *Enterprises*, and asks around for a fast ship. Data states that the *Enterprise* maxes out at just shy of Warp 10, but that doesn't mean anything to a man used to blasting his way through hyperspace.

"In how many parsecs can she do the Kessel Run?" Obi-Wan asks.

While Data tries to explain that a parsec is a unit of distance, not time, Picard comes in to confront the intruder. Kenobi waves a hand at Picard and then points to Data. He says, "That's the droid you're looking for."

The strong-willed Picard ignores the Jedi mind trick and summons security to deal with the situation. Kenobi offers to buy Picard a drink, but this gesture means nothing at a bar at which the drinks are all free. It all goes bad when Lieutenant Worf puts a hand on Kenobi. Ben's lightsaber leaps out, and Worf loses an arm.

Picard calls for the ship's computer to wall off the part of the bar that Kenobi's in with a force field. Stumped for a moment, Kenobi slices through the floor instead and disappears into the lower levels of the ship.

RESULT: Draw—for now.

THE RASH YOUNG MEN

Most science fiction shows feature a rash young man the fans can identify with. He's often the viewpoint character for much of the shows or films that include him, and he tends to have a mentor he's destined to supplant, affirming the natural order of things—or at least the status quo.

LUKE SKYWALKER VS. COMMANDER RIKER

LUKE SKYWALKER

OCCUPATION: Farm boy yearning to see the galaxy

DATAPOINT: Mark Hamill first stepped into the role of Luke Skywalker in *Star Wars: A New Hope* at the age of twenty-five.

SNAPSHOT: Luke is a whiny kid who's been itching for years to leave his sandy home of Tatooine behind. When the aunt and uncle who raised him are killed, he decides it's time to finally grow a pair and strike out to find his destiny. Despite the fact that he's possibly the most powerful Jedi since his father, he has almost zero training and is more likely to hurt himself with his father's lightsaber than save the galaxy.

COMMANDER WILLIAM RIKER

OCCUPATION: Starship first mate—sorry, "officer"

DATAPOINT: Jonathan Frakes, who played Commander Riker in *Star Trek: The Next Generation*, is eleven months younger than Mark Hamill.

SNAPSHOT: When he accepts his commission as Captain Picard's first officer on the newly christened *Enterprise-D*, Riker is a young man going places fast, and he's just hit his peak. He turned down his own command so that he could serve under Picard on the *Enterprise*, apparently not realizing or caring that that would mean he'd have to wait for Picard to either retire or die until he had another chance at his own ship.

WHO'D WIN?

Commander Riker beams down to Mos Eisley for a bit of R&R and is delighted to discover he's stumbled into a wretched hive of scum and villainy. While he's boozing it up at an unnamed cantina, a young farm boy bumps into him and spills his drink all over Riker's freshly pressed uniform. When Riker insists that Luke apologize and bring him a new drink, Luke panics. He gave all his money, including the title to his landspeeder, to Obi-Wan Kenobi and can't find the old man anywhere.

Still unwise in the ways of the Force and never having done more than wave his hand-me-down lightsaber back and forth, Luke goes for his blaster rather than his blade. As a trained combatant, Riker stops Luke cold, strips him of his weapon, and tosses it aside.

Unwilling to surrender, Luke attacks Riker, but the older, better-trained man knocks the farm boy flat. Afterward, Riker dusts off his hands, winks at a bug-eyed alien he assumes is female, and orders another round for himself and the young man on the floor.

RESULT: Riker delivers a commanding win for Star Trek.

THE SCOUNDRELS

Not every leader goes by the rules. Some, instead, run their ship by the seat of their pants, relying on their skill, ingenuity, and sheer dumb luck. These are people who are only too happy to bluff, cheat, or lie their way through a problem when no other way will work. Only when those options have been exhausted do they resort to weapons—or fists.

HAN SOLO VS. CAPTAIN KIRK

HAN SOLO

OCCUPATION: Scoundrel

DATAPOINT: Han was the star of one of the first series of Star Wars novels, beginning with 1979's *Han Solo at Stars' End* by Brian Daley.

SNAPSHOT: Han Solo is a professional smuggler with a long history of avoiding any Imperial entanglements. Along with his copilot, Chewbacca, who owes Han a life-debt, he's modified his ship, the *Millennium Falcon*, until it's become the fastest freighter in the galaxy. Solo's seen a lot in his day, and the first thing he's learned is that rules are for suckers when the Empire's writing the rulebook. Recently, Jabba the Hutt placed a price on Solo's head for dumping his precious cargo rather than being arrested by the Empire, making Solo desperate to make enough cash to save his skin.

CAPTAIN JAMES T. KIRK

OCCUPATION: Starship captain

DATAPOINT: James T. Kirk was born on March 22, 2233, in Riverside, Iowa.

SNAPSHOT: When James T. Kirk takes over the *Enterprise* from its previous captain (Pike), he's a tender thirty-one years old, the youngest person to ever be given command of a Federation starship, not to mention a vessel as large and important as the *Constitution*-class heavy cruiser USS *Enterprise*. Having proved himself a top student at Starfleet Academy, he accelerated through Starfleet's ranks by a combination of smarts, skill, and sheer inventiveness, along with his refusal ever to admit defeat.

Cocky doesn't begin to describe his level of self-confidence.

WHO'D WIN?

Captain Kirk meets Han Solo in Docking Bay 94 of the Mos Eisley spaceport. Solo and Chewbacca have been going over the *Millennium Falcon*, making sure it's ready for a quick getaway. They know that Jabba has a price on their heads, so they're nervous about strangers wearing uniforms.

Kirk knows a smuggler when he sees one. He enters the bay with an away team of red shirts ready to back his play. Solo sees them and sends Chewie into the ship while he parlays with Kirk.

Under other circumstances, Kirk and Solo might hit it off, but Kirk's away team is twitchy, and Solo's suspicious of anything in a uniform, even if he doesn't recognize it. As soon as the red shirts raise their phasers, Solo leaps to the side, and Chewie opens up with the *Falcon*'s belly gun.

Kirk manages to dodge the blasts, but the red shirts get mowed down. In the chaos, Solo dashes into the ship before Kirk can retaliate, and a moment later the *Millennium Falcon* races away, leaving Kirk scowling up after it.

RESULT: Solo edges out Kirk here, though he doesn't beat Kirk so much as evade him. If we're talking about the Special Edition version of Solo, Kirk might be able to take him out, but real fans stick with the original version in which Solo would win—because *Han shoots first.*

EARLIER LEGENDS

Before they became the kinds of legends whose stories are bandied about the entire galaxy, every leading man had to start somewhere. Every story has a beginning. Some even have prequels, and some of those prequels have heroes of their own.

These men served as mentors to or heroes of the people in the original tales. They helped form the original stories, even if they never appeared in them or were only mentioned in passing, but they have stories of their own that deserve to be heard too.

QUI-GON JINN VS. JONATHAN ARCHER

QUI-GON JINN

OCCUPATION: Jedi Master

DATAPOINT: Fans first encountered Qui-Gon in the movie *Star Wars: The Phantom Menace*, which premiered on May 19, 1999.

SNAPSHOT: Qui-Gon isn't your Jedi's Jedi. Though a powerful and influential man, he's a loose cannon who encourages his padawan (student) Obi-Wan Kenobi to trust his instincts rather than remove all emotion from his life. He could have been part of the Jedi Council, but he clearly wouldn't want to be a part of any club that would have him.

JONATHAN ARCHER

OCCUPATION: Starship captain

DATAPOINT: Archer took command in the *Star Trek: Enterprise* pilot episode "Broken Bow," which first aired on September 26, 2001.

SNAPSHOT: Archer is already a legend when he's made the captain of the first starship capable of reaching Warp 5, the *Enterprise (NX-01)*. As a test pilot, he's dreamed of exploring space for years, and now he finally has his chance. He's not going to let anything stop him.

Nothing ever has.

WHO'D WIN?

Archer encounters Qui-Gon while exploring Naboo, and the Jedi immediately takes Archer and his ship to be minions of the Trade Federation, there to capture or kill Queen Amidala. He draws his lightsaber to warn Archer off, but the Federation captain doesn't scare so easily. He draws his phaser and fires.

Qui-Gon deflects the phaser beam with his lightsaber. It takes him a moment to realize it's a beam rather than a bolt, but that doesn't fool him into lowering his guard. Instead, he angles his lightsaber to reflect the beam back at Archer.

Anticipating this, Archer lets his finger off the trigger and dodges away. Even Archer can't outrun a beam of nadion particles traveling at the speed of light, though, and the beam catches him and knocks him unconscious. Good thing he had it set on stun.

RESULT: Qui-Gon delivers a stunning victory.

SEASONED VETERANS

There's a moment in time when a man has already come of age but he's not ready to be shuffled off to the old heroes home (or a teaching job at the Jedi Academy or Starfleet Academy) quite yet. He's in his prime and is ready for any kind of challenge, whether he knows it or not. The specter of his ultimate destiny still looms far over him, but he can ignore that for now and do his best to be the hero he once was—and hopes he can be again.

ANAKIN SKYWALKER VS. BENJAMIN SISKO

ANAKIN SKYWALKER

OCCUPATION: Jedi Knight

DATAPOINT: A total of four actors—Hayden Christensen, Jake Lloyd, Sebastian Shaw, and Matt Lanter—have played Anakin Skywalker (not counting his Darth Vader years).

SNAPSHOT: Having served as Obi-Wan Kenobi's padawan, Skywalker is a full-on Jedi Knight who's already become a hero of the Republic. He's struggling to master his emotions, though, as his frustrations with the galaxy around him mount.

BENJAMIN SISKO

OCCUPATION: Starfleet commander

DATAPOINT: Actor Avery Brooks, who portrayed Sisko in *Star Trek: Deep Space Nine*, was born in Evansville, Indiana, in 1948.

SNAPSHOT: As the recently appointed commander of a space station inherited from the Cardassians, Sisko's head whirls with cataloging and analyzing the various factions vying for fortune, power, or freedom in the newly discovered Gamma Quadrant. He considered resigning from Starfleet instead of taking this job, but instead he's learning to come to terms with his wife's death at the hands of the Borg, his status as a single father, and the puzzling fact that he might just be the Emissary of the Prophets—godlike aliens that live in the Bajoran wormhole.

WHO'D WIN?

Anakin arrives on Deep Space Nine on a mission the Jedi Council assigned to him. He doesn't understand it, and the fact that the elder Jedi consistently keep him in the dark grates on his nerves. He growls enough at the service in Quark's Bar that Quark calls Sisko down to "greet" the newcomer.

When Sisko arrives, Skywalker has Quark by the ear and is accusing him of trying to rip him off. "You're worse than the filthy Jawas!" he says to the agonized Ferengi.

Sisko walks in and orders Skywalker: "Take your hands off that Ferengi!"

Skywalker's hand goes to his lightsaber, but he doesn't draw it yet. "I'm tired of taking orders," he says.

"Fine," Sisko replies, putting up his hands. "Then let me order you—a drink." He gestures for Quark to bring a bottle of Romulan ale.

Skywalker accepts the gesture grudgingly and sips the potent drink. Not wishing to show weakness, he forces himself to drain his glass. A moment later, he collapses to the floor, drugged asleep.

"You know that stuff's illegal," says Quark.

"So what did you really feed him?" says Sisko.

Quark rubs his bruised ear. "Enough tranquilizers to keep him out for a week."

RESULT: Chalk up a win for Sisko, who used his head when Anakin led with his battered heart.

OUR RUNNING TALLY

Leading Men

	SAGA THIS CHAPTER	RUNNING TALLY
Star Wars	2	2
Star Trek	2	2
Ties	1	1

Both sagas get off to a solid start here, which isn't much of a surprise. They both have fantastic leading men, after all. At the end of Chapter 1, it's a solid tie.

How much do you know about the women in the two series? Or were you blinded by their galactic beauty? Really?

1. **The name of the planet that Princess Leia gives to Grand Moff Tarkin to try to keep him from destroying Alderaan is:**
   A. Dantooine   C. Hoth
   B. Yavin   D. Naboo

2. **The actress who played Tasha Yar is the granddaughter of:**
   A. Ronald Reagan   C. Bob Hope
   B. Gene Roddenberry   D. Bing Crosby

3. **Ahsoka Tano's nickname for her master is:**
   A. Darth Tedious   C. Ani Banani
   B. Skyguy   D. Mom

4. **Nyota Uhura's first name was officially revealed in:**
   A. *Star Trek: The Original Series*
   B. *Star Trek: The Motion Picture*
   C. *Star Trek: Generations*
   D. *Star Trek (2009)*

5. **One of Queen Amidala's handmaidens often pretended to be her to act as a decoy in case of trouble. Her name was:**
   A. Sabé
   B. Rabé
   C. Leia
   D. Saché

6. **Seven of Nine's original name was:**
   A. Seven of Seven
   B. Alice Janeway
   C. Annika Hansen
   D. Ophelia Scott

Answers: 1. A, 2. D, 3. B, 4. D, 5. A, 6. C

CHAPTER 2

WOMEN
More Than Just Pretty Faces

While the men of Star Wars and Star Trek may have started out with the main roles, women have come on strong in the intervening decades. In Star Wars, they've gone from princesses who need to be rescued to queen-senators who rule wisely and well and are handy in a gunfight. In Star Trek, they've advanced from nurses and communications officers all the way up to captains of starships of their own.

Still, the managers of each franchise have never been afraid to play up the sex appeal of their women. Princess Leia didn't wind up in that skimpy slave girl outfit in Jabba's palace by accident, and Kirk always went for the pretty girls, no matter their planet of origin. And Borg or not, Seven of Nine's bodysuit had no scientific reason to be so tight.

And women have embraced the sexy side of science fiction too. At the last few San Diego Comicons, a bevy of beautiful women dressed in Leia's slave girl uniform gathered for a group photo-op around a life-sized model of Jabba the Hutt.

Still, we're not grading the women of Star Wars and Star Trek by their beauty alone. For our contest, they'll have to stand up and fight!

THE INGÉNUES

Just because you're powerful doesn't mean you know what you're doing. When power comes to you too young, or when you've led a sheltered life, you can seem like a babe in the woods compared to the more seasoned alien-fighters around you. Sometimes, just like your male counterparts, say Luke Skywalker or Wesley Crusher, your only hope is to find a capable teacher who can help you live up to your potential.

PADMÉ AMIDALA VS. SEVEN OF NINE

PADMÉ AMIDALA

OCCUPATION: Democratically elected queen of Naboo

DATAPOINT: Natalie Portman, who first played Padmé in *Star Wars: The Phantom Menace*, was born Natalie Hershlag in Jerusalem, Israel.

SNAPSHOT: When Padmé Amidala became the queen of Naboo at the tender age of thirteen, circumstances thrust her immediately into war with the Trade Federation. Compelled to flee her homeworld rather than be captured, she had little experience of the wider galaxy. Despite her sheltered upbringing, Amidala enjoyed the protection of two Jedi (Obi-Wan Kenobi and Qui-Gon Jinn) and the services of a large retinue of handmaidens, some of whom resembled her enough to serve as decoys for her when necessary.

SEVEN OF NINE

OCCUPATION: Borg refugee

DATAPOINT: Jeri Ryan, who played Seven of Nine in *Star Trek: Voyager*, made her debut acting appearance in an episode of *Who's the Boss?*

SNAPSHOT: Captured and assimilated into the Borg Collective at the tender age of six, Seven of Nine spent eighteen years as a

Borg. When she was trapped on the Federation starship *Voyager,* the Starfleet crew managed to separate her from the collective. Soon after, the Doctor managed to remove most of her Borg circuitry, leaving only the most vital of her Borg implants still in place. She knows little of the ways of humanity after so much time as part of the Borg, and she trusts no one.

WHO'D WIN?

Seven of Nine beams down into the Theed Royal Palace on Naboo and finds Queen Amidala in her throne room, surrounded by her handmaidens.

Thinking that Seven is a cyborg representative of the Trade Federation, Amidala orders her handmaidens—who also serve as her bodyguards—to attack. The young women throw themselves at Seven in a concerted attack.

Unfortunately, Seven easily repels the handmaidens. Her Borg implants make her faster and stronger than any normal human, and while she may not know how to curtsy before a queen, she can certainly take one apart.

Surprised by Seven's resilience, the handmaidens rally back to their queen's side, hoping to sell their lives as dearly as possible and buy their mistress's other protectors enough time to come to her rescue. Unimpressed, Seven methodically tears through the women until she reaches the queen and hoists her up into the air by her neck.

It's then that the woman Seven of Nine thought was Queen Amidala is revealed to be an impersonator named Sabé. Queen Amidala's spies learned of Seven's impending visit—and disagreeable temper—and evacuated their queen to safety.

Seven is unimpressed, but she restrains herself from killing the imposter. Maybe she's been living with free, unaltered humans for too long.

RESULT: Almost a draw, but I'll give this one to Seven. Given enough time, she'd find Amidala and tear her apart too.

WARRIOR WOMEN

Being a warrior may not be the most ladylike of professions, but it's not just men who prefer to stand up for themselves instead of letting someone else handle it for them. The right women can be some of the toughest and hardest fighters in the galaxy. Let's pick a pair of warriors at different points in their careers and pit them against each other to see what happens.

AHSOKA TANO VS. CAPTAIN KATHRYN JANEWAY

AHSOKA TANO

OCCUPATION: Jedi Padawan

DATAPOINT: Actress Ashley Eckstein provides the voice of Ahsoka in the movie and TV series *Star Wars: The Clone Wars*.

SNAPSHOT: The young Ahsoka Tano is the youngest Jedi Padawan ever. Raised in the Jedi Academy since the age of three, Ahsoka is cocky and overconfident, certain she can take on just about anything. When she was promoted to padawan, Yoda made her the apprentice to Anakin Skywalker. She adores Anakin and calls him "Skyguy," for which he dubbed her "Snips."

CAPTAIN KATHRYN JANEWAY

OCCUPATION: Starship captain

DATAPOINT: Canadian actress Geneviève Bujold was originally cast as Captain Janeway in *Star Trek: Voyager*, but luckily for Kate Mulgrew, things didn't quite work out.

SNAPSHOT: While there were other female captains in the Federation, Kathryn Janeway was the first to be prominent enough to be featured in her own show, *Star Trek: Voyager*. Sadly, in the first episode of the show, her ship was tossed into the Delta Quadrant, about 70,000 light-years away from the Federation. Janeway is a tough, fair, and accomplished captain who has seen battle before.

She is determined to bring her people back to their home in the Alpha Quadrant or die trying.

She may get her wish.

WHO'D WIN?

Ahsoka is racing through space on a diplomatic mission when her hyperspace computer goes wonky and hurls her so far off course that she winds up in the Delta Quadrant. When she stumbles upon *Voyager* there, she decides that a gigantic warship like that can't be any good. Before she can flee back home though, *Voyager* captures her ship in its tractor beam and hauls it aboard.

Once inside, Ahsoka is dragged off to the bridge. Janeway insists on knowing who she is and where she came from, but Ahsoka's not about to talk with anyone outside of the Old Republic for fear of being branded a traitor. She pulls her lightsaber and charges into battle.

After Ahsoka nearly dismembers a few of the bridge crew and displays herself unwilling to listen to Janeway's pleas, the captain decides she has no choice. Grabbing the transporter controls herself, she beams Ahsoka back to her own ship and sends her on her way. Captain Janeway doesn't have time for petulant padawans.

RESULT: Janeway wins.

THE BEAUTIES

Smart, gorgeous, and capable, some heroines seem to have it all. Their only real problem is finding a mate capable of keeping up with them, which is never an easy task. Because of that, they can seem a bit stand-offish at times, too used to having to fend off advances to leave themselves open for a real relationship. Eventually someone perseveres and wins her heart, but until then . . .

LEIA ORGANA VS. NYOTA UHURA

LEIA ORGANA

OCCUPATION: Interstellar diplomat, spy, and princess of Alderaan

DATAPOINT: Carrie Fisher, who played Leia from *Star Wars: A New Hope* onward, is the daughter of Hollywood royalty Eddie Fisher and Debbie Reynolds.

SNAPSHOT: Leia Organa is as sharp-tongued and feisty as they come. Having no idea that she's the daughter of Darth Vader, she has worked with her adoptive father, Senator Bail Organa, to further the cause of the Republic in its efforts to resist Emperor Palpatine's efforts to destroy it. To that end, she has been willing to risk life, limb, and freedom to fight for what she believes is right, and tough luck to anyone who stands in her way.

NYOTA UHURA

OCCUPATION: Starfleet communications officer

DATAPOINT: The role of Uhura, made famous in the original series by Nichelle Nichols, was taken over by Zoe Saldana for *Star Trek (2009)*.

SNAPSHOT: As one of the most promising students in Starfleet Academy, Uhura is determined not to allow anything—or any*one*— to get in her way. She meets a young James Kirk in a bar on Earth, just before she ships out, but he doesn't impress her a bit. She can see right through his reckless ways and instead takes up with one of the most intelligent and ambitious men she's ever met: a Vulcan named Spock. Despite her romantic entanglements, Uhura is determined to stand on her own. She studies as hard as anyone and earns her place on the *Enterprise*.

WHO'D WIN?

Princess Leia wanders into a bar in Iowa that's packed with Starfleet cadets about to be shipped out of the Academy. James Kirk hits on her first thing, but she affects her frostiest British accent and blows him off so coldly he nearly freezes to the floor. When Kirk rallies, Leia tears into him, declaring that she won't ever be tempted to fall for some brainless flyboy.

But Kirk doesn't believe in the no-win scenario, and eventually Leia pulls a blaster from her belt and points it at him. As Kirk backs away, linguist Uhura's sense of outrage at Leia's inconsistent accent rises to a boiling point, and she steps forward to knock the blaster out of Leia's hand.

Furious, Leia throws herself at Uhura. The two engage in a battle of nail scratches and hair pulling that soon has the men in the bar cheering them on.

Irritated by this, the two women spiral away from each other and smash into the men instead, kicking and shouting at them until they run screaming from the establishment. When Uhura turns to slap Leia a high five, she's rewarded with a blast to the chest from Leia, who took advantage of the commotion to recover her pistol. Fortunately, Leia decided she liked Uhura enough to set the weapon to stun.

RESULT: Leia's barely suppressed rage outweighs Uhura's finely tuned ear.

THE YOUNG LADIES

Let's face it. Not all the women of Star Wars and Star Trek serve as models of the modern, progressive woman. Sometimes they just give the rest of the cast someone to shelter and protect. As individuals, they may be smart, capable people, but that only makes the plots centered around them that much more sinister.

SABÉ VS. NURSE CHAPEL

SABÉ

OCCUPATION: Royal handmaiden and decoy

DATAPOINT: Future movie star Keira Knightley played Sabé in *Star Wars: The Phantom Menace*, cast for her uncanny resemblance to Natalie Portman.

SNAPSHOT: Sabé has been raised to be a royal handmaiden from a young age. Her resemblance to Queen Amidala makes her the perfect stand-in for times when circumstances require the queen to shield herself from danger. While she can communicate secretly with Amidala via silent hand gestures, Sabé knows she can never truly fill the queen's robes.

NURSE CHAPEL

OCCUPATION: Starfleet nurse

DATAPOINT: Actress Majel Barret, who played Chapel in *Star Trek: The Original Series*, played four more roles in various Star Trek incarnations.

SNAPSHOT: Nurse Chapel is a dedicated Starfleet officer and a key member of Dr. McCoy's staff on board the *Enterprise*, but she's also a woman. She's the consummate professional, but still finds herself drawn to the aloof Mr. Spock, a Vulcan she knows can never love her the way a human could.

WHO'D WIN?

Beaming down to Naboo, Nurse Chapel finds herself in the antechamber of a royal throne room as Sabé is about to receive representatives from the Trade Federation. Surprised by Chapel's appearance, Sabé responds just as she's been trained to. She presents herself as the queen of Naboo, and demands to know who has trespassed in her private antechamber.

Nurse Chapel apologizes, while surreptitiously giving the young woman the once-over with her medical scanner. Based on data from the transporter's bio-filter, Chapel knows this isn't really the queen, and she palms a tranquilizing hypospray.

But Sabé sees the hypospray and, thinking it's a weapon, connects with a vicious kick to Chapel's chin that knocks her flat.

RESULT: Sabé's training as part of the royal bodyguard carries the day.

THE EXOTICS

While most of the leading roles in the Star Wars and Star Trek sagas went to humans, a number of aliens have also had featured roles. Alien ladies can often intrigue some viewers with their exotic good looks and repel others with their alien natures.

After all, there's nothing quite like ogling a blue-skinned hottie only to realize that her funky hairstyle is actually a pair of tails growing out of the top of her head. Or finding out that the beautiful and accomplished science officer is actually a symbiont whose other half is an ancient, sluglike creature who's already lived several lifetimes, both male and female.

It might be enough to make you want to stay single.

AAYLA SECURA VS. JADZIA DAX

AAYLA SECURA

OCCUPATION: Jedi Knight

DATAPOINT: Aayla is one of the few characters in the series first created for a comic book (*Star Wars: Republic: Twilight*) who made it into the movies (*Star Wars: Attack of the Clones*).

SNAPSHOT: In the early days of the Clone Wars, Separatist forces capture Obi-Wan Kenobi on the planet Geonosis. As a newly knighted Jedi, Aayla joins a large Jedi strike team in an attempt to rescue Kenobi. Though inexperienced in the ways of war, she fights well, always maintaining control, and proves herself worthy of being a Jedi Knight.

JADZIA DAX

OCCUPATION: Starfleet science officer

DATAPOINT: Terry Farrell played Jadzia Dax in the first six seasons of *Star Trek: Deep Space Nine*. She then starred opposite Ted Danson in *Becker*.

SNAPSHOT: Being joined with Dax allows Jadzia to emerge from her shell and become a confident and sexy woman at ease with herself and the world around her. Jadzia is not immortal, but Dax is, and that dichotomy permeates everything the two do together.

WHO'D WIN?

While charging through the canyons in Geonosis, Secura becomes lost. Hoping to catch up with the rest of the Jedi so that she can stand with them against the Separatists, she instead runs into Jadzia Dax, who came to explore the wonders of the worlds on the other side of the Bajoran wormhole. Apparently, she should have taken that last turn at Ceti Alpha Six.

Dax hears Secura coming, and she pulls her phaser. Spying Dax as she rounds a corner, Secura activates her lightsaber. Dax fires her phaser, but Secura deflects it away.

Dax fires again, this time at the rocks over Secura's head. Huge boulders come tumbling down at the young Jedi, but she catches them with the Force and hurls them at Dax instead, walling her into an igloo of broken stones.

RESULT: Chalk one up for the Jedi, but Dax's memory is long, and you can bet the next encounter will be different indeed.

OUR RUNNING TALLY

Leading Women

	SAGA THIS CHAPTER	RUNNING TALLY
Star Wars	3	5
Star Trek	2	4
Ties	0	1

With the leading women, Star Wars takes its first lead. While there aren't as many female characters in Star Wars as there are in Star Trek—and not as many characters of any kind, to be honest—the ones they have are spectacular and really stand out.

QUIZ 3

Whether their foreheads are bumpy, they've got antennae, or they look like big walking carpets, what do you know about aliens?

1. **Boba Fett's father was:**
   A. Darth Vader
   B. Jango Fett
   C. Papa Fett
   D. Mace Windu

2. **Worf was the first Klingon to:**
   A. Marry a Romulan
   B. Serve with Starfleet
   C. Declare himself a vegetarian
   D. Sing karaoke

3. **Chewbacca's favored weapon was called a:**
   A. Bowcaster
   B. Crossblaster
   C. Wookiee rifle
   D. Ballaster

4. **Spock was half human, which came from:**
   A. His mother, Christine Chapel
   B. His father, Sybok
   C. His mother, Amanda Grayson
   D. His father, Jonathan Archer

5. **Dr. Evazan, the man who picked a fight with Luke Skywalker in the Cantina at Mos Eisley, had the death sentence in how many systems?**
   A. Six
   B. Five
   C. Thirty
   D. Twelve

6. **T'Pol was the first Vulcan to:**
   A. Serve with Starfleet
   B. Marry a Romulan
   C. Have an emotion
   D. Meet a human

Answers: 1. B, 2. B, 3. A, 4. C, 5. D, 6. A

CHAPTER 3

ALIENS
No Need to Phone Home

Aliens are one of the signal hallmarks of science fiction. As soon as you see an eight-foot-tall hairy monster stride across the screen with a bowcaster strapped across his back, you know you're not in Kansas any more. Andorians may have blue skin, a shock of white hair, and antennae, but they're our neighbors in the United Federation of Planets.

Both Star Wars and Star Trek are chock full of creatures from way beyond anywhere on planet Earth. Some of them may look like humans with funky facial ridges, but it takes more than simply adding a few subdermal facial bones to make an alien.

The best aliens show us something about ourselves. They highlight some aspect of human nature, like the gluttony of the Hutts or the Vulcans' desire for control, that show up in every one of us. Even the strangest aliens often show us something we can identify with, like the whimper of a dying Rancor and the tears its keeper sheds over it.

THE TOUGH GUYS

Talk about tall, dark, and dangerous, the toughest aliens are the ones you want on your side in the middle of a fight. It doesn't matter if they're next to you in the cockpit or if they've got your back in a firefight, you'd much rather be *with* them than *against* them. And even though they may be gentle giants once you get to know them, you'll still want to let them win at dejarik.

CHEWBACCA VS. WORF

CHEWBACCA

OCCUPATION: Starship mechanic and first officer

DATAPOINT: Author R. A. Salvatore received death threats when fans read of Chewbacca's death in his novel *Star Wars: The New Jedi Order: Vector Prime.*

SNAPSHOT: At nearly 200 years old, Chewbacca's seen a lot of the galaxy and the dangers it has to offer. This Wookiee is officially retired from soldiering at the moment and has partnered up as a smuggler with his friend Han Solo. Hopping the spacelanes from one wretched hive of scum and villainy to another beats living under the oppressive rule of the Empire, even if it means having to do business with people like Jabba the Hutt.

A loyal and capable friend, Chewie stands ready to do anything he can to protect those he cares about. As for the occasional Imperial Stormtrooper, he's prepared to rip their arms off if that's what it takes.

WORF

OCCUPATION: Starfleet lieutenant

DATAPOINT: Michael Dorn starred as Worf in both *Star Trek: The Next Generation* and *Star Trek: Deep Space Nine.*

SNAPSHOT: Worf survived the Khitomer Massacre at the hands of the Romulans only to be found by Sergey Rozhenko, who brought the young Klingon orphan home to his wife to raise him as their son. Worf became the first Klingon to join Starfleet, and he worked hard to earn a post on the *Enterprise*. He is determined to prove himself and to find a way to integrate his Klingon heritage with the Federation culture in which he was raised.

Despite the humanizing effects of his upbringing, Worf can be a brutal warrior. He often advocates action over diplomacy and bristles at his *Enterprise* crewmates' hesitance to spill a little blood.

WHO'D WIN?

Worf is drinking by himself at the bar in the Mos Eisley Cantina when Chewbacca shoulders his way up to place an order with the bartender. The Wookiee nudges the Klingon aside, accidentally spilling Worf's bloodwine.

"You will apologize for that!" Worf says as he stands up.

Chewbacca looks down at the Klingon and gives him a noncommittal growl.

"A weakling apology like that is not enough!" Worf says, his nostrils flaring. "You will also buy me a new drink!"

Chewbacca growls again.

"Of course I understand you," Worf says. "My universal translator is working fine. Your ears, however, must be plugged. You will buy me a drink!"

Chewbacca turns his back on Worf and orders a drink for himself and Han Solo. Worf punches him in the back. *"Ha'DlbaH!"* the Klingon says. "I demand satisfaction!"

With an irritated growl, Chewbacca spins around and grabs Worf by the wrists. He then spreads his arms apart in a hard, fast move that separates both of Worf's shoulders at once. As the Wookiee continues to pull at the growling Klingon's arms, a voice from behind him gives him pause.

"Chewie!" Han Solo shouts from across the Cantina. "Quit playing with your little friend there and get over here. We got business to take care of!"

RESULT: Chewbacca by an arm's length.

THE LITTLE ONES

Aliens come in all shapes and sizes, but it's the little ones that seem to surprise us the most. As humans, we're trained to think of smaller bipeds as children: innocent, carefree, and harmless. But when it comes to aliens, that misperception can prove dangerous. Size has nothing to do with how deadly something can be.

NIEN NUNB VS. KES

NIEN NUNB

OCCUPATION: Smuggler, rebel, copilot

DATAPOINT: The language Nien speaks in *Star Wars: Return of the Jedi* is a combination of the Kenyan dialects Haya and Kikuyu.

SNAPSHOT: As a Sullustan, Nien Nunb grew up in the underground caves of his home planet, forging his way through the darkness. After Sullust supported the Empire, he worked against it as a smuggler. During that time, he met and became friends with Lando Calrissian.

When it came time for the Rebel Alliance to launch an assault against the Death Star II, Nunb joined Calrissian as his copilot on the *Millennium Falcon*, which they'd borrowed from Han Solo. Nien is confident that he and Lando can do their part in the battle, but he worries whether the others can manage theirs.

KES

OCCUPATION: Medical assistant, USS *Voyager*

DATAPOINT: Jennifer Lien played the role through *Star Trek: Voyager*'s fourth-season episode "The Gift."

SNAPSHOT: Over the three years she's been on *Voyager*, Kes has grown up a lot. That's only natural for an Ocampa, for whom the expected lifespan is just nine years. At the moment, she's hitting middle age for her kind.

Kes's telekinetic powers have been increasing over the years. She fears that they might progress beyond her ability to control, and she is afraid she could threaten the safety of everyone aboard.

WHO'D WIN?

Nien Nunb enters one of the outposts of the Mikhal Travelers, hoping to find something he can smuggle back to Sullust under the nose of the Empire. He has his wide, mousy eyes on several barrels of Toffa ale he figures he can sell at a huge profit back home. Unfortunately, Kes wants them as well.

"I'll take them all," Nunb says to the Mikhal merchant.

"You can't do that," Kes says, distressed at the thought that she won't be able to bring Neelix back some of his favorite drink. "I can't find this anywhere else. Believe me, I've looked."

"Exactly why I want it," Nunb says, putting his arm around Kes. "You wouldn't want me to disappoint my customers, would you?" He smiles as best he can with his Sullustan mouth.

"I only need one barrel," Kes says as she looks down at him. "Surely you can spare that?"

"Of course," Nunb says, stabbing a thumb at the merchant. "If you can meet his outrageous price, be my guest."

Kes grins in delight, but her face falls as she reaches for the supply of gold-pressed latinum she'd brought with her to pay and finds that it's gone. As she races off to find it, Nunb pulls the valuable element from behind his back and arranges to take all of the Toffa ale off the merchant's hands.

RESULT: Nunb. Those Sullustan smugglers sure are sneaky.

THE LEADERS

Just as is true with humans, the power of many aliens lies not in their incredible strength or their ability to manipulate the Force but in the others they have allied around them. Even a Jedi Knight must think twice before taking on an entire army by himself. (Maybe with two of them, sure, but it's a bigger risk alone.)

Few aliens are singularly unique. Most hail from planets filled with their own kind, and the more persuasive of them can ally with species from the farthest reaches of space.

ADMIRAL ACKBAR VS. LOCUTUS OF BORG

ADMIRAL ACKBAR

OCCUPATION: Military commander of the Rebel Alliance

DATAPOINT: Students at the University of Mississippi have petitioned to make Admiral Ackbar their football team's mascot.

SNAPSHOT: As a Mon Calamari, Ackbar grew up on the world of the same name, which provided many of the Rebel Alliance's greatest warships. Having proved his skills as a military leader, Ackbar rocketed through the ranks of the Rebel forces. He is about to face the biggest challenge of his stellar career: designing the attack on the Imperial base on Endor and the simultaneous attempt to destroy the Death Star II.

Ackbar is brilliant at coming up with daring plans. He only worries about how he can possibly make it all come together with the Rebel Alliance's limited resources.

LOCUTUS OF BORG

OCCUPATION: Borg press secretary

DATAPOINT: Picard was assimilated in the *Star Trek: The Next Generation* two-part episode "The Best of Both Worlds."

SNAPSHOT: Locutus of Borg was once Captain Jean-Luc Picard of the *Enterprise*, now having been assimilated into the Borg Collective. Rather than giving orders and taking responsibility for how they're carried out, Locutus has only to play his role in the Borg hive mind. Despite the fact this means killing many Starfleet officers, he feels no remorse, only the shared satisfaction that the assimilation of the survivors is inevitable.

WHO'D WIN?

While Admiral Ackbar is waiting to head for Endor with his Rebel forces, his ship, *Home One*, picks up a distress signal from the *Enterprise*. Before he can even respond to this unknown vessel, a Borg cube pops out of Warp right in front of his fleet. Locutus of Borg hails him, and Ackbar opens voice communications with him.

"Surrender your ships, and prepare to merge your biological distinctiveness to the collective," Locutus says. "Resistance is futile."

"It's a trap!" Ackbar shouts.

Recognizing this code phrase, the Rebel ships begin evasive maneuvers. Several of them fire on the Borg cube. The first few damage the cube, but the Borg force shield automatically reconfigures itself to render the massive ship invulnerable to further attacks.

"We don't have time for this!" Ackbar shouts. "All ships! Make the jump to hyperspace, now!"

Within seconds, every one of the Rebel ships disappears into hyperspace. Unable to track them, the Borg decide to resume their course toward Wolf 359.

RESULT: The Borg take this one by forfeit. Resistance may be futile, but running away at least delays the inevitable.

ALIEN SLAVE GIRLS

Some alien races still enslave other races, whether as a source of cheap labor or for some other evil purpose. For some reason, some of the most notable slaves in both universes are green-skinned females who don't wear much clothing. These ladies perform many services, of course, but their primary function appears to be serving as eye candy—at least until their masters tire of them.

OOLA VS. MARTA

OOLA

OCCUPATION: Dancer, slave to Jabba the Hutt

DATAPOINT: The actress behind the Oola makeup, Femi Taylor, also danced her way through the role of Tantomile in *Cats*.

SNAPSHOT: Oola is not having a good life. Kidnapped from her home planet of Ryloth, the poor Twi'lek girl was trained as an exotic dancer and brought to Jabba's palace to serve as entertainment for him and his guests. Oola would like nothing better than to choke Jabba to death with her chains, but she fears his wrath too much to attempt it. She hopes that if she pleases him enough, Jabba might one day let her go. Yeah. What are the chances of *that* happening?

MARTA

OCCUPATION: Asylum occupant, slave girl

DATAPOINT: Incarcerated in the *Star Trek: The Original Series* episode "Whom Gods Destroy," the actress Yvonne Craig who played Marta was also familiar to fans of TV's *Batman* as Batgirl.

SNAPSHOT: Marta has also had a hard life. As a female Orion, she was supposed to be sold to a male whom she would then control with her powerful pheromones. Instead, she wound up in a Federation asylum on Elba II, unable to use her wiles on anyone.

Despite her beauty, she's afraid she's past her prime now and is desperate for male attention that she can turn to her own designs.

WHO'D WIN?

Bib Fortuna arrives at the asylum and kidnaps Marta, bringing her to entertain at Jabba's palace. When he brings Marta and Oola before Jabba, the Hutt crime lord proclaims that he has too many lovely dancers to keep track of at once. He declares that they will have a dance-off—to the death!

Oola uses her home field advantage to signal Max Rebo and his band to play her a tune she knows well. She whirls and dances until her green skin and headtails are slick with sweat. When she finishes, Jabba gives her an appreciative chortle.

When the music for Marta starts, she realizes she doesn't know the tune. Fearful that she cannot compete with Oola fairly, she releases her most powerful pheromones, directing them at Jabba, hoping to gain his favor. As the scent reaches him, though, Jabba recognizes what Marta is trying to do.

Offended that Marta would try such a cheap ploy with him, Jabba rages at her until she backs up onto the trap door in the center of the room. He then signals for it to drop Marta into the Rancor's pit, and he proceeds to enjoy her final show.

RESULT: Oola, who knew better than to try cheap mind games on a Hutt.

LOGIC AND WISDOM

Some aliens just seem smarter than the rest of us, although it's hard sometimes to tell if that's because everyone of their species is so brilliant or you were just lucky enough to bump into their Einstein. Either way, there are different kinds of brilliance. Vulcans, for instance, rely on logic alone—or so they like to say. Figures like Yoda, on the other hand, try to impart the hard-earned wisdom that comes with his advanced age. Others, like Q, seem like fools, but in the end it often turns out that he's far smarter than he lets on.

Let's pit a couple of them against each other and see who's at the top of the class and who's just a wise guy.

YODA VS. SPOCK

YODA

OCCUPATION: Jedi Master, outlaw

DATAPOINT: Voice Yoda, filmmaker and Muppeteer Frank Oz did.

SNAPSHOT: Having been a Jedi Master for nearly 900 years now, Yoda is tired. After surviving Order 66, which massacred most of the other Jedi, he hid on Dagobah, where he's waited out his twilight years in obscurity and filth. And now Anakin's son has gone off to battle Darth Vader, without even knowing who he is. So much for any new hope.

SPOCK

OCCUPATION: Starfleet science officer

DATAPOINT: In 1977 Leonard Nimoy wrote an autobiography entitled *I Am Not Spock,* but he finally surrendered in 1995 with the follow-up *I Am Spock.*

SNAPSHOT: Spock has found it easier to fit in among his fellow Starfleet officers than he first expected. While they had their own prejudices against him at first, he is now able to count several of them as friends. Sometimes this causes him to question the Vulcan way of strict emotional control, but his logic never fails him.

WHO'D WIN?

An away team led by Mr. Spock beams down to Dagobah to investigate signs of recent starfighter activity. One by one, the red-shirted officers he brought with him are eaten by some of the native fauna. As Spock ponders his next move, Yoda approaches him.

"Belong here you do not," Yoda says. "Leave you must."

"Highly illogical," Spock says as he scans Yoda with his tricorder. "You are intelligent but willingly violate the rules of grammar to make yourself seem wiser than you are. An interesting contradiction."

"Control your emotions you must," Yoda says, poking his staff at Spock, "or lose yourself to the Dark Side you will."

Spock raises an eyebrow. "My emotions are under better control than yours. I am only trying to rescue you from this hostile swamp."

"Do or do not. There is no try."

Spock opens up his communicator. "Two to beam up." He looks down at Yoda. "Place my guest here in the brig."

Yoda gasps. "Not necessary is tha—!"

RESULT: Spock, whose logic triumphs over wise riddles.

OUR RUNNING TALLY

Aliens

	SAGA THIS CHAPTER	RUNNING TALLY
Star Wars	3	8
Star Trek	2	6
Ties	0	1

Again, Star Wars gets a small edge here, increasing its lead. Both series have a number of great alien races. Fewer of the ones in Star Wars, though, look like people united by a common facial oddity, and that may have made the difference.

Every society needs "minions," the worker-bees of both universes. But how much do you really know about them?

1. **The Clone Troopers were clones of:**
   A. Jango Fett
   B. Obi-Wan Kenobi
   C. Qui-Gon Jinn
   D. Grand Moff Tarkin

2. **In *Star Trek: The Original Series*, crew members wearing red shirts were part of:**
   A. The science division
   B. The command division
   C. The engineering and support services division
   D. The short-timers' club

3. **The Sand People of Tatooine were also known as:**
   A. Jawas
   B. Banthas
   C. Genoshans
   D. Tusken Raiders

4. **During the Battle of Wolf 359, Jean-Luc Picard fought for the Borg as:**
   A. Locutus of Borg
   B. Elocution of Borg
   C. Picard of Borg
   D. One of Seven

5. **The pig-faced, green-skinned guards at Jabba's palace hail from:**
   A. Mos Eisley
   B. Gamorr
   C. Xindi
   D. Dantooine

6. **The Jem'Hadar are a genetically engineered race that has no:**
   A. Females
   B. Sense of smell
   C. Sense of fear
   D. Toes

Answers: 1. A, 2. C, 3. D, 4. D, 5. B, 6. A

CHAPTER 4

MINIONS
Someone's Got to Do the Dirty Work

What would the powerful in Star Wars and Star Trek be without someone to boss around? Or to die in their stead to show us how dangerous the galaxy can be, demonstrating just how hard the heroes must have to work to survive? When you need faceless characters with few if any lines to fill those roles—or countless loyal troops—it's time to call in the minions.

We've seen some of the big names from each universe face off against each other. Now let's see how their support teams stack up.

THE CANNON FODDER

Sometimes it seems like a minor character's only reason for being is to give the more important people in the story someone to shoot at. After all, the bad-asses of the story have a hard time intimidating anyone if they can't cause any harm. That's where the cannon fodder come in: mostly nameless folk who might be just as brave or competent as any of the stars in the tale but who just aren't destined for anything other than their fifteen seconds of on-screen fame.

STORMTROOPERS VS. RED SHIRTS

STORMTROOPERS

OCCUPATION: Soldiers in the Imperial Army, cannon fodder

DATAPOINT: As many as fifty different specialties of stormtroopers blast their way through the expanded Star Wars universe.

SNAPSHOT: The stormtrooper program began with the rise of the Galactic Empire and sprang from the clone trooper initiative begun under the then chancellor Palpatine during the Clone Wars. Many of the stormtroopers are also clones, though a good number of them may also be planetary recruits that share the clones' complete loyalty to the Empire. They obey orders without question, no matter the risk to themselves, and rigorously follow the Imperial chain of command.

RED SHIRTS

OCCUPATION: Starfleet security officers, doomed souls

DATAPOINT: More than 70 percent of the Starfleet characters who died in the third season of *Star Trek: The Original Series* wore red shirts.

SNAPSHOT: The red-shirted men and women of Starfleet Security are just like any other Federation officers. Tough, well-trained, and armed with state-of-the-art phasers, these security personnel may have a lower survivability rate than the average Starfleet officer, but they knew the risks when they signed on.

WHO'D WIN?

An away team beams into the Death Star to see if they can figure out why no one is answering the *Enterprise*'s hails. As a group of five red shirts appears in the center of the main hangar, a squad of stormtroopers spots them and rushes over to accost them.

"Hold it right there," the lead stormtrooper says as he and his fellows level their blaster rifles at the red shirts.

Knowing a hostile enemy when they see one, the red shirts open fire with their phasers. One of them has the presence of mind to reach for his communicator to request they be beamed out of there, but while looking over his shoulder as he flees, he falls into a bottomless pit that has no good reason to be there.

The stormtroopers keep the red shirts on the run, but they can't seem to hit any of them with a blaster bolt, despite filling the air in the hangar with glowing bits of light. The red shirts manage to take out a few of the stormtroopers with their phasers, but as soon as one of the men in white goes down, another steps up to take his place.

RESULT: It's a tie. Really, it could go on forever, and the camera cuts away long before that.

WAR PIGS

Every villain needs someone to do his dirty work for him. Often these are feckless and cruel soldiers whose only real qualifications are their innate brutality. Star Wars and Star Trek have plenty of examples of these unsavory sorts. But what happens if we pit them against each other rather than against the heroes?

GAMORREANS VS. JEM'HADAR

GAMORREANS

OCCUPATION: Guards at Jabba's palace

DATAPOINT: The traditional war axe of the Gamorreans is called an *arg'garok*.

SNAPSHOT: These porcine, green-skinned brutes hail from Gamorr, a world still technologically stuck in the distant past. Because of that, these large, dim-witted thugs still prefer battle-axes to blasters, though they can point and shoot if someone shoves a blaster into their hands.

JEM'HADAR

OCCUPATION: Dominion shock troops

DATAPOINT: These soldiers were introduced, along with the Vorta, in the season-two finale of *Star Trek: Deep Space Nine*: "The Jem'Hadar."

SNAPSHOT: The Jem'Hadar are genetically engineered, force-grown soldiers who are kept loyal to their creators by means of a congenital addiction to ketracel-white, a drug the Founders control. Built to be aggressive and independent, yet honorable, they would prefer to be free, but they worship their creators like gods and have yet to figure out a way to rebel against them.

WHO'D WIN?

A squad of five Jem'Hadar soldiers land outside of Jabba's palace and storms its way in. The Gamorrean guards at the gate put up some resistance but are killed with their battle-axes still in their hands. The door holds just long enough for the Gamorreans inside to switch to their blasters before it explodes inward.

The Jem'Hadar First orders the others to fan out and take the Gamorreans down. The Gamorreans try to make use of the winding, dark passageways in the palace to try to surprise the invaders, but they're too large and unwieldy to pull it off.

The Jem'Hadar suffer a single casualty when one of the Gamorreans hurls an axe at the Third and catches him in the chest. When the remaining Jem'Hadar reach Jabba's inner chambers, they find the Hutt waiting for them, ready to cut a deal.

RESULT: The Jem'Hadar take this in a walk. The Gamorreans may be soldiers too, but the Jem'Hadar were literally made for this.

STEEL SOLDIERS

One of the most frightening things on any field of battle is a foe who never gets tired and never relents, coming at you over and over like a machine. It's that much worse if your enemies *really are machines*.

Both Star Wars and Star Trek have their own kinds of killing machines, creatures that keep fighting for as long as their energy and ammunition hold out. But what happens if we program them to relentlessly attack each other?

B1 BATTLE DROIDS VS. THE BORG

B1 BATTLE DROIDS

OCCUPATION: Soldiers

DATAPOINT: CGI armies of B1 battle droids first took to the field of battle in *Star Wars: The Phantom Menace.*

SNAPSHOT: The Trade Federation launched the first battle droid army with its invasion of Naboo. The spindly, mindless warriors performed perfectly, overwhelming the people of Naboo with superior firepower and numbers. They don't display anything in the way of initiative, but with an excellent tactician behind them, they can prove unstoppable.

THE BORG

OCCUPATION: Assimilation

DATAPOINT: Their first taste of Federation biological distinctiveness came in the *Star Trek: The Next Generation* episode "Q Who?"

SNAPSHOT: Like the battle droids, the Borg are mindless warriors controlled by a central intelligence. But unlike battle droids, not all of a Borg's body is made up of metal. The robotic components are fused to a living host that's been assimilated into the Borg Collective by means of those implants. The Borg are relentless fighters, and their total lack of personal individuality makes them willing to sacrifice themselves without regret so that the rest of the Collective can learn from their demise.

WHO'D WIN?

As a battalion of battle droids marches across the hills of Naboo on the way to the capital city of Theed, a Borg cube appears in orbit and starts beaming Borg down to the planet's surface. The Borg do not speak to the droids. They recognize them as nothing more than machines, and machines by themselves do not interest the Collective because they cannot be assimilated. Instead, the Borg unleash their phasers at the battle droids and mow them down.

The droids respond in full force and destroy the first wave of Borg. The Collective quickly learns from this destruction though and modifies the shields of the next wave of Borg to protect it from the battle droids' weapons. Unable to respond in kind, the battle droids find their weapons useless, and the Borg blast them to pieces.

Then the Collective turns its eyes toward its real prize: Theed.

RESULT: The Borg outmatch the battle droids at every level.

SAVAGES

Not every fighting force is known for its strict adherence to the chain of command or for the honorable way in which it conducts itself. Some of them are just packs of savage maniacs trying to beat the snot out of the other side before the other side can beat the snot out of them. They can be fearsome foes, especially in close quarters. Line them up a mile away though, and you can just pick these berserkers off one at a time before they reach you.

But what would happen if you tossed two of these mobs into the same tight place?

TUSKEN RAIDERS VS. NAUSICAANS

TUSKEN RAIDERS

OCCUPATION: Nomads, raiders

DATAPOINT: Tusken Raiders spurred Anakin Skywalker toward the Dark Side of the Force when they kidnapped and killed his mother in *Star Wars: Attack of the Clones.*

SNAPSHOT: The Tusken Raiders—a.k.a. Sand People—are nomadic natives of the desert planet Tatooine. Wandering its sandy wastes, the Sand People are so hostile that no outsiders claim to have ever seen a live one outside of its distinctive, bandagelike wrappings. Tusken Raiders rarely come close to human settlements, but when they do, blood is always spilled.

NAUSICAANS

OCCUPATION: Thugs, pirates, and hired muscle

DATAPOINT: Q gives Picard a second shot at the Nausicaans in the *Star Trek: The Next Generation* episode "Tapestry."

SNAPSHOT: The Nausicaans are tall, muscled brutes who take what they like and hire themselves out to others willing to give them what they want. They tend to drink and gamble away what money they have, so that the cycle of mercenary violence is continuously replenished. Three Nausicaans nearly killed young Ensign Jean-Luc Picard in a bar fight, and Picard still has the artificial heart to remind him of their ill-tempered ways.

WHO'D WIN?

A crew of Nausicaan pirates celebrates a recent success by tearing up a seedy bar out on the edge of Anchorhead on Tatooine. They're in the middle of a heated game of dom-jot on which a lot of credits are riding when a pack of Tusken Raiders bursts into the place, intent on killing everyone inside and stealing everything they can carry off.

The first two Nausicaans near the door go down with the business ends of a pair of gaderffii sticks in their chests. The remaining Nausicaans respond with relish. They've been itching for a chance to bruise their knuckles since they arrived here, and now they're finally going to get it.

That turns out to be the Nausicaans' fatal error. If they'd gone for their phasers, they might have been able to make quick work of the Tusken Raiders. As it is, the bar stools and dom-jot cues can't stand up to the Tuskens' gaderffiis. In under a minute, the Nausicaans are all dead, and the Raiders are picking through the wreckage the battle made of the bar.

RESULT: The Tusken Raiders put the heads of the Nausicaans on pikes.

MINION LEADERS

Some of those low on the chain of command still manage to distinguish themselves. They may not ever rise to the ranks of heroes, win any ribbons, or have any movies made about them, but they make up a good part of the tale's supporting cast.

At the very least, they're listed in the credits by name rather than just "Thug #1," or "Mutant on Motorcycle."

CLONE CAPTAIN REX VS. CHIEF ENGINEER OLSON

CLONE CAPTAIN REX

OCCUPATION: Captain of the Republic's clone army

DATAPOINT: The captain takes command in the movie *Star Wars: The Clone Wars.*

SNAPSHOT: As part of the 501st Clone Trooper Battalion, Unit CC-7567 served directly under General Anakin Skywalker during the Clone Wars. Despite being one of the clones of Jango Fett, he is exceptionally strong willed. As a loyal servant of the

Republic, he always follows his orders but won't hesitate to express his opinion when it's called for. Rex is able to establish and maintain friendships with people outside the inner circle of clone troopers, notably Anakin Skywalker and his padawan Ahsoka Tano.

CHIEF ENGINEER OLSON

OCCUPATION: Starfleet officer, chief engineer on the *Enterprise*

DATAPOINT: Actor Greg Ellis appeared twice in *Star Trek: Deep Space Nine* before taking on the role of Olson in J. J. Abrams's *Star Trek (2009)*.

SNAPSHOT: The headstrong Chief Olson became first chief engineer aboard the *Enterprise* NC-1701 on its maiden voyage to help investigate an attack on the planet Vulcan. Thrilled to have achieved such a fantastic accomplishment at such a young age, he believes he's invincible. He loves nothing better than a thrill, and he expects his career in Starfleet to be full of them. If there's a hero in the story, then it's clearly meant to be him.

Too bad the chief engineer wears a red shirt.

WHO'D WIN?

Chief Engineer Olson beams down to the surface of Kamino during the middle of a battle. Captain Pike wants a detailed assessment of the enemy's technological capabilities. Olson was only too eager to volunteer for the duty. Because he wants to impress his captain, he insists on being beamed down into the thick of things rather than to a safe observation point on the edge of the action.

Olson appears before Captain Rex as the commander is racing toward his old barracks, which is under fire from Separatist forces. Olson raises his phaser and demands the clone troopers identify themselves.

Seeing that Olson is not wearing clone trooper armor, doesn't appear to be a Jedi, and clearly isn't a Kaminoan, Rex raises his twin blaster pistols and opens fire. The other clones bring up their blaster rifles and join in.

This is a little more action than the engineer bargained for. As he calls for help, Olson gets off one phaser shot that stuns one of the unnamed clone troopers. Then the *Enterprise* beams Olson back aboard a split second before Rex's shots would have caught Olson square in the chest.

And their blasters were *not* set on stun.

RESULT: Olson gets schooled. Chalk up this one for Captain Rex.

OUR RUNNING TALLY

Minions

	SAGA THIS CHAPTER	RUNNING TALLY
Star Wars	2	10
Star Trek	2	8
Ties	1	2

This chapter's a tossup. Both sagas have some excellent grunts in their ranks, the kind that just about anyone involved with American culture would recognize in a heartbeat. A tie feels right, but Star Wars maintains its lead.

Who's trying to take over the galaxy? Or at least a corner of it? And what do you know about them?

1. **Darth Vader's voice was supplied by:**
   A. Samuel Jackson
   B. Don LaFontaine
   C. Patrick Stewart
   D. James Earl Jones

2. **In *Star Trek (2009)*, Nero is:**
   A. Romulan
   B. Ferengi
   C. Bajoran
   D. Wookiee

3. **Before he became Emperor, Palpatine was also known as:**
   A. Darth Bane
   B. Darth Sidious
   C. Yoda's apprentice
   D. King of Naboo

4. **Captain Kirk marooned Khan and his crew on:**
   A. Rigel
   B. Earth
   C. Ceti Alpha V
   D. Remus

5. **The leader of the Separatists was:**
   A. Darth Maul
   B. Nute Gunray
   C. Queen Amidala
   D. Jar-Jar Binks

6. **The Grand Nagus, leader of the Ferengi Alliance, was:**
   A. Zek
   B. Quark
   C. Rom
   D. Kahless

Answers: 1. D, 2. A, 3. B, 4. C, 5. B, 6. A

CHAPTER 5

VILLAINS
You Can't Have a Saga
Without Them

The most memorable characters in any story are the ones we love to hate, the villains who work their way into our collective subconscious and become part of our modern myths and legends. Thoughts of their evil acts stir all sorts of emotions in our own hearts and keep us up at night as we ponder the inhumanity of them, and our own resolve to stand fast against dark temptation.

And damn, are they cool.

THE KILLERS

The villains that startle and shock us aren't the ones that *threaten* to kill—they just go ahead and do it. They're not in it for the money or power, they just want someone dead, and they're prepared to do whatever it takes to get the job done.

It's hard to defend against this sort of bad guy because he doesn't stop to deliver a soliloquy about how the heroes had it coming, or leave behind puzzles to help himself get caught. He just hits it and quits it as hard as he can.

DARTH MAUL VS. NERO

DARTH MAUL

OCCUPATION: Sith apprentice

DATAPOINT: Like fellow Sith Lord Darth Vader, Darth Maul was played by two actors: Ray Park (in person) and Peter Serafinowicz (voice).

SNAPSHOT: Darth Maul is the apprentice of Darth Sidious, and at the time we first meet him, the two of them are the only members of the Sith still in existence. Maul is expected to grow in power until he's strong enough to challenge and kill Sidious, but he's not quite ready to attempt that yet. And he'll die before his chance comes.

Maul is a stone-cold killer so chilling he barely says a word. He lets his deadly actions—and his double-bladed lightsaber—speak for him.

NERO

OCCUPATION: Miner, captain, instrument of revenge

DATAPOINT: Actor Eric "Nero" Bana admitted to being a Trekkie even before he stepped onto the set of *Star Trek (2009)*.

SNAPSHOT: Nero is a bereaved Romulan who blames Spock for failing to save the planet Romulus—and Nero's pregnant wife—from destruction. He has traveled into the past to find a way to save Romulus and exact revenge on both halves of Spock's heritage: human and Vulcan. He cares little about anything else, allowing his heartbreak and rage to drive him to ever more heinous acts of genocide.

WHO'D WIN?

Maul is sent to steal Nero's planet-busting red matter for Darth Sidious's own nefarious plans. To that end, Maul flies a small fighter straight into the *Narada* and then leaps off his own ship at the last moment. Landing with his double-bladed lightsaber out and ready, Maul begins his final hunt for Nero.

For his part, Nero doesn't care about Darth Maul or any of the Sith. All he wants is revenge. If he dies after he attains that, he'll go happily at least. He sends his men to attack Maul until he can get his ship close enough to attack Vulcan.

Maul slices through Nero's Romulan crew at an alarming rate, stalking closer and closer to Nero himself. Eventually, he runs out of other people in his way, and he moves in for the kill. In a last-ditch attempt to take his hated enemies with him at least, Nero releases the red matter to destroy Vulcan. Maul uses the telekinetic powers of the Force to capture and contain a single drop of red matter and flees the collapsing *Narada*. As he makes the jump to hyperspace, Maul wonders if he might have finally found what he needs to kill Darth Sidious and take over as Lord of the Sith.

RESULT: Darth Maul cuts Nero's strings.

THE COMMANDERS

Remember all those minions in the last chapter? Who do you think pushes them all around like pieces on a tridimensional chess board? Their commanders, of course.

These villains may have a plan, but they depend on motivating others to do their dirty work for them. They may stand on the field of battle, but they prefer to run their operations from the rear so they can change tactics as needed and even, if necessary, flee from the face of defeat so they can plague the heroes again another day. After all, you can't keep a good villain down for long.

COUNT DOOKU VS. GENERAL CHANG

COUNT DOOKU

OCCUPATION: Separatist leader, Sith apprentice

DATAPOINT: Dooku once served as Qui-Gon Jinn's mentor, as recounted in the young reader novel *Star Wars: Legacy of the Jedi* by Jude Watson.

SNAPSHOT: Having instigated the Clone Wars and fully committed himself to Darth Sidious as a Sith apprentice named Darth Tyrannus, Dooku enjoys prosecuting the Separatist side of Palpatine's plans. This battle-scarred ex-Jedi hopes to soon realize his dream of crushing the corrupt Republic and the order of the Jedi along with it. At the moment, no one seems to have a prayer of stopping him, and because of this, his arrogance grows apace with his power.

GENERAL CHANG

OCCUPATION: Klingon chancellor's chief of staff

DATAPOINT: The Shakespeare-quoting Chang was played by *The Sound of Music* star Christopher Plummer in the movie *Star Trek VI: The Undiscovered Country*.

SNAPSHOT: Despite the fact that he does not bear the cranial ridges or coloration of most members of his race, Chang is a Klingon's Klingon. He believes in the supremacy of his people and in the honor that comes from battle. He refuses to consider peace with the Federation, even though it seems inevitable. Few would be as audacious as he in coming up with a plot to prevent peace— much less have the skills and knowledge to successfully pull it off—but Chang is a rare Klingon in many ways.

WHO'D WIN?

Searching for more allies to help spread chaos across the Republic, Dooku approaches Chang and proposes an alliance. "There is flattery in friendship," Chang responds, "but the Klingon Empire does not wish to ally with humans. We stand ready, instead, to fight them."

Realizing he's made a mistake, Dooku draws his lightsaber and brandishes it before him, daring Chang to attack. Chang smiles.

"There's no trust, no faith, no honesty in men; all perjured, all for-sworn, all naught, all dissemblers."

"I think I've heard enough," Dooku says. "You will give me free passage from here."

"Or?"

In reply, Dooku fries Chang half to death with Force lightning. "Or," Dooku says, "I can make that hurt much worse."

Chang calls for his guards to save him, but Dooku uses the Force to seal the doors and shocks Chang again. "The quality of mercy is not strain'd," Chang croaks.

"I have no idea what you're babbling about," Dooku says. With that, he turns to stalk his way out through the ship.

RESULT: Dooku never really gave Chang a chance.

THE HIDDEN FOES

The blows you never see coming are often more devastating than the ones you do. It's one thing for a hero to have to be on his guard against enemies who openly declare their evil intentions, but it's another thing entirely to be forced to be wary of everyone around you in case there's a traitor in your midst just waiting for his chance.

DARTH SIDIOUS VS. DR. TOLIAN SORAN

DARTH SIDIOUS

OCCUPATION: Sith Lord, Chancellor of the Republic

DATAPOINT: Sidious finally takes his revenge in *Star Wars: Revenge of the Sith.*

SNAPSHOT: Darth Sidious has worked for years to get to this point, playing both sides of the Clone Wars against each other to further his own personal ambitions for ultimate control of the entire galaxy. Now he's finally ready to toss aside his carefully constructed facade and declare himself Emperor. After all, at this point, there's no one who could stop him—at least not for a good twenty-three years.

DR. TOLIAN SORAN

OCCUPATION: Scientist

DATAPOINT: He actually had a hand in killing the previously un-killable Captain Kirk in the movie *Star Trek: Generations*.

SNAPSHOT: After Dr. Tolian Soran lost his entire family and most of the population of his homeworld El-Aurian to the Borg, his refugee ship had a brief brush with the Nexus, a strip of white light that formed a gateway into a timeless sort of heaven. Soran is a cunning schemer and an accomplished liar, willing to do anything and sacrifice anyone to attain his goal. His current plan will murder millions of people if it succeeds.

WHO'D WIN?

Soran approaches Darth Sidious to acquire the Republic's gravity generator technology, which it sometimes employs as part of an interdict field that prevents ships in its field from jumping to hyperspace. Soran hopes to use this to influence the path of the Nexus energy ribbon so that he can enter it. In exchange, he will not reveal to the galaxy that Sidious is actually Palpatine.

Sidious counters Soran's offer with a liberal dose of Force lightning that drives the scientist to his knees.

"Give me one reason why I should not kill you now," Sidious says.

Soran smiles through the pain. "Because I've recorded this entire incident and broadcast it to my ship via subspace. If I do not stop it within the hour, it will rebroadcast the recording to every member of the Galactic Senate."

Sidious helps Soran to his feet. "Well played," he says. "But if I give you what you want, what assurance do I have that you will not expose me then?"

"My dear Sidious," Soran says, a mad glint in his eyes. "If I succeed, I will be far beyond caring about what happens to you and your plans for Empire."

RESULT: Soran blindsides Sidious by outthinking him at every turn.

THE OUTCAST LEADERS

The most dangerous villains are those evil leaders that come from outside of the current societal and political structures but know how to work within it. While they have the means to manipulate larger organizations or governments to their own aims, they don't have any basic values in common with those they're influencing. That means they're willing to sacrifice anyone and anything at any point to further their personal agendas.

GENERAL GRIEVOUS VS. SHINZON

GENERAL GRIEVOUS

OCCUPATION: Military leader for the Confederacy of Independent Systems, Jedi hunter

DATAPOINT: Fans still argue over whether or not Grievous's organic parts were retrieved from the body of Sith apprentice Darth Maul.

SNAPSHOT: Grievous was once a great Kalee warrior, but after he suffered horrible injuries, most of his body outside of his essential organs was replaced with bionics. Though he resembles the droids from the Separatist army he leads, a heart beats somewhere inside his metal carapace. As he heads into the Battle for Coruscant, Grievous hopes to add to his collection of trophy lightsabers he's stripped from the Jedi he's killed.

SHINZON

OCCUPATION: Revolutionary and mass murderer

DATAPOINT: The character was played by actor Tom Hardy in the 2002 movie *Star Trek: Nemesis*. Hardy later appeared in the movie *Inception*.

SNAPSHOT: The ambitious clone of Jean-Luc Picard survived the Reman mines to claw his way to the top of the Romulan military. Desperate to find and kill Picard for a life-saving blood transfusion, Shinzon plans to take over the Romulan Senate so he can make a temporary peace with Picard. He then means to betray Picard and destroy the Federation, cementing Romulus as the Alpha Quadrant's supreme power.

WHO'D WIN?

Shinzon contacts General Grievous and requests an audience so that he can demonstrate his thalaron generator, a weapon that can kill every living thing on the planet. Thinking that such a tool would be a perfect complement to his droid army, Grievous decides to welcome the clone's visit.

When Shinzon's ship—the *Scimitar*—meets up with Grievous's starship, Shinzon beams onto Grievous's bridge. He carries a lightsaber, which he offers to Grievous as a gift. Always to the point, Grievous asks what Shinzon wants in exchange for his technology.

"Only justice for the clone army you face," Shinzon says, a mysterious smile on his lips. "Nothing more."

Grievous accepts Shinzon's offer. "You will witness its effects today," Shinzon says just before he beams away.

Confused by what Shinzon meant, Grievous decides to try his new lightsaber. When activated, though, it emits greenish particles instead of a glowing blade. Within seconds, these eat their way through his protective organ sack. The general howls in horror as his last remaining living parts crumble into dust.

RESULT: Shinzon's thalaron-infused lightsaber trap never gave Grievous a chance.

THE LEGENDS

Every saga has its legendary villains, the ones who send shivers down your spine when they appear onscreen. The dread music swells, the camera pulls in tight, and the galaxy seems to tremble. These people prove the focus of the heroes' greatest battles, the foes they cannot hope to defeat but must somehow still find a way.

The best of these villains are just as three-dimensional as the heroes, complete with their own complex and understandable motivations. If they have a great voice that can ring out withering threats too, then all the better.

DARTH VADER VS. KHAN

DARTH VADER

OCCUPATION: Dark Lord of the Sith, Emperor Palpatine's apprentice and right-hand man

DATAPOINT: Vader really begins to scheme in the space between the movies *Star Wars: The Empire Strikes Back* and *Star Wars: Return of the Jedi.*

SNAPSHOT: Anakin Skywalker never planned to become a Sith Lord, but he's too far gone now to turn back. His recent reunion with his son, Luke, didn't go as well as he'd hoped and gave him much to chew over. If he could only come up with a way to defeat the Emperor, he might be able to take the throne himself and finally make everything better.

KHAN NOONIEN SINGH

OCCUPATION: Genetically engineered superman, dictator

DATAPOINT: Khan first appeared in the *Star Trek: The Original Series* episode "Space Seed" in 1967 and was rediscovered fifteen years later for the movie *Star Trek II: The Wrath of Khan.*

SNAPSHOT: Khan knows himself to be superior to all humans. He was engineered that way, after all. But now, after so many years trapped on the hellish wasteland of Ceti Alpha V, he wants nothing more than revenge on Kirk. He's stolen the starship *Reliant*, and now his vengeance is close enough he can taste it, and he'll have it, even if he has to stab at Kirk from Hell's heart, chase him through the Antares maelstrom, or sacrifice his entire crew.

WHO'D WIN?

Khan spies the Death Star II and, fearing Kirk may be hiding within, flies the *Reliant* toward it. The space station catches the hijacked Federation ship in a tractor beam and hauls it in. When the stormtroopers board the ship to arrest the occupants, Khan and his people overpower them and take their weapons. They then begin a rampage through the ship, planning to kill whomever they must so that they can wrest control of the massive weapon for Khan, who plans to use it to bend the entire Federation to his superior will.

Surprised by the audacity and savagery of Khan's attack, Darth Vader goes to personally put an end to it. He meets Khan in the Emperor's vacant control room and reaches out to choke him with the Force. Refusing to panic, Khan holds his breath and charges straight at Vader, tackling him to the floor and tearing off his helmet.

As Khan gasps at the sight of Vader's true face, Vader rallies and uses the Force to lift Khan into the air and pin him against the giant observation window. Khan struggles to throw some *Moby Dick* quotes at Vader, but the Sith Lord just tosses him to the side like a genetically superior rag doll.

RESULT: Darth Vader wouldn't have let himself be marooned in the first place.

OUR RUNNING TALLY

Villains

	SAGA THIS CHAPTER	RUNNING TALLY
Star Wars	3	13
Star Trek	2	10
Ties	0	2

Star Wars gets the edge again. The series has so many iconic villains that it's almost surprising it didn't dominate more, but Star Trek has a few insanely memorable baddies, too. That kept things close.

QUIZ 6

You have two huge universes to choose from, and there are plenty of things to know about their occupants. Show us what you've got!

1. **Han Solo is from the planet:**
   A. Tatooine
   B. Coruscant
   C. Endor
   D. Corellia

2. **Captain James T. Kirk's last works were:**
   A. "It was ... fun. Oh my..."
   B. "Never give up. Never surrender!"
   C. "I don't believe in the no-win situation."
   D. "Khaaaaannn!!!"

3. **The natives of the planet Kashyyyk are called:**
   A. Ewoks
   B. Betazoids
   C. Wookies
   D. Dugs

4. **The galactic power that held sway over most of the Gamma Quadrant was known as:**
   A. The Dominion
   B. The Alliance
   C. The Foundation
   D. The Empire

5. **Anakin Skywalker is destined to become:**
   A. Obi-Wan Kenobi
   B. Darth Vader
   C. Emperor Palpatine
   D. Jar-Jar Binks

6. **Wesley Crusher was last officially seen:**
   A. As the President of the Federation.
   B. Accompanying the Traveler to parts unknown.
   C. Attending the wedding of Will Riker and Deanna Troi.
   D. Headlining W00tstock.

Answers: 1. D, 2. A, 3. C, 4. A, 5. B, 6. B

CHAPTER 6

POWERS
What Makes the Galaxy
Go Round

The true powers in any galaxy are the ones that go beyond reasonable personal gain and aspire to rule large swathes of the galaxy. Some of these powers cannot be killed with a single phaser beam or a swipe of a lightsaber's blade. If you remove an organization's figurehead, after all, another usually steps up to take its place, and then you're right back where you started, maybe worse off than before.

But that doesn't mean you shouldn't try.

THE EMPIRES

The greatest power in a galaxy is rarely in the hands of a single being. Instead, true power lies in the empires built by countless hands and supported by billions more. Whether they spread across just a portion of a galaxy or the entire thing, they form a force unstoppable by anything less than a dedicated alliance of freedom fighters.

Empires aren't built overnight nor are they quick to fall. When they clash against each other, though, the sparks that fly burn like supernovas.

THE GALACTIC EMPIRE VS. THE KLINGON EMPIRE

THE GALACTIC EMPIRE

OCCUPATION: The ruling power in most of the galaxy

DATAPOINT: Established in the year 19 BBY, the Galactic Empire begins about a year before the start of *Star Wars: A New Hope.*

SNAPSHOT: Palpatine formed his Empire by building the Separatist movement into a phantom menace that would terrify the Republic Senate into handing over supreme power to him. He has ruled over the galaxy with an iron fist for the past eighteen years, and only the pathetic Rebel Alliance stands in his way. That's what worries him. Should he destroy the pesky Alliance, what then?

He needs a new menace.

THE KLINGON EMPIRE

OCCUPATION: To rule over all Klingons and as much of the rest of the galaxy as they can conquer

DATAPOINT: This version of the Klingon Empire is as it appeared around the time of the movie *Star Trek II: The Wrath of Khan.*

SNAPSHOT: The Klingon Empire and the United Federation of Planets have been lumbering through a cold war and toward peace for years. Unable to gather support for a full-out invasion of the Federation, some factions within the Klingon Empire are itching for a new foe to fight, despite Chancellor Gorkon's reservations.

They're about to find one.

WHO'D WIN?

When a Klingon Bird-of-Prey is captured in Imperial space, an intrigued Emperor sends the surviving members of the crew back home with a holocron message that ends, "We're coming."

Chancellor Gorkon uses this to stir the High Council into frenzy, and the Klingons gear up for war. When the Empire doesn't invade right away, Gorkon decides he must make a pre-emptive strike or risk having the squabbling Klingons fall into a civil war.

The invasion goes well at first, and the Klingons take a few worlds on the Galactic Rim, including Tatooine. The Emperor uses this news to whip his own people into a fury. The Rebels temporarily abandon their attacks against the Empire to help fight against the greater perceived threat from another universe. The Klingons relish the battles fought against their increasingly tougher foes, but they're shocked into subjugation after the Death Star blows Qo'noS to pieces.

And from there, the Emperor Palpatine's gaze turns toward the Federation.

RESULT: The Galactic Empire crushes the much smaller Klingon Empire in a way no other foe ever has.

THE EXTERIOR THREAT

Nothing moves a people to join together and fight side by side better than to face a common foe. Sometimes these threats come from a newly formed faction that had until now lain unseen, but other times they hail from distant reaches of the galaxy, or even alternate universes.

THE CONFEDERACY OF INDEPENDENT SYSTEMS VS. THE DOMINION

THE CONFEDERACY OF INDEPENDENT SYSTEMS

OCCUPATION: Separatist movement fighting against the Republic, unsuspecting tool of Chancellor Palpatine

DATAPOINT: This confederacy appears in season one of *Star Wars: The Clone Wars*.

SNAPSHOT: Under the leadership of Count Dooku, the various guilds and corporate elements of the Separatist movement have permanently allied themselves with each other to form the

Confederacy of Independent Systems. They seek to bring down the Republic and set up a much looser—and more easily controlled—government in its place.

Sadly, they just don't know how dangerous a place the galaxy really is.

THE DOMINION

OCCUPATION: Domination of the Gamma Quadrant and conquerors of all else

DATAPOINT: The Dominion retreated back to the Gamma Quadrant after the final season of *Star Trek: Deep Space Nine*.

SNAPSHOT: The Dominion just fought a devastating war in the Alpha Quadrant against the Federation Alliance, but circumstances forced it to go back to the Gamma Quadrant. The Founders who rule the Dominion must now turn their attention elsewhere or risk having the Dominion eat itself from within. To that end, they turn their gaze beyond their galaxy.

WHO'D WIN?

The Confederacy forces have their hands full dealing with their rebellion against the Republic. They're not looking for more trouble, but it comes looking for them in the form of the Dominion.

The Dominion discover a lost smuggling ship in the Gamma Quadrant and reverse-engineer its engines to develop a hyperspace drive. Tapping into the navigational computers on the derelict ship, they plot a route to Tatooine and from there to the Republic's core systems.

When the Dominion arrives, it is in force, with a complete navy of Jem'Hadar warships. They take Tatooine down fast and move on to Geonosis, where Count Dooku sends his forces to make a stand. The Jem'Hadar warriors tear through the droid forces, breaking the Confederacy's spine and scattering its supporters to the corners of the galaxy.

And from there, it's only a short hyperspace jump to Coruscant. But forewarned now, Palpatine is ready.

RESULT: The Dominion de-confederates the Separatist movement.

THE POLITICIANS

One sort of amassed power is worse than the nastiest, messiest, most corrupt sort of organization ever dreamed up by any Ferengi or Hutt. I speak, of course, of politics. As stories go, politics don't amount to nearly as much action as a good lightsaber duel or a starship battle, but they can often offer up just as much drama. At the least, politics help give any other situation a broader context and show how the results of more personal dramas can affect huge swathes of people.

Consider it a necessary evil.

THE GALACTIC SENATE VS. THE FEDERATION COUNCIL

THE GALACTIC SENATE

OCCUPATION: Overseeing the laws, planets, and people of the entire galaxy—or at least those not part of the Separatist movement

DATAPOINT: Although it was first mentioned in *Star Wars: A New Hope*, we didn't get to see the Senate assembled until *Star Wars: The Phantom Menace*.

SNAPSHOT: Under the guidance of Supreme Chancellor Finis Valorum, the Galactic Senate struggles to remain coherent in the face of many threats, not the least of which is the Separatist movement being launched by the Trade Federation. Hamstrung by bureaucrats, Valorum often feels like little more than a figurehead for the vast government he's been elected to oversee. The constant bickering over conflicting self-interests means the Senate doesn't get much done on most days, but perhaps that's for the best.

THE FEDERATION COUNCIL

OCCUPATION: Governing body of the United Federation of Planets

DATAPOINT: You can read the full text of the Articles of Federation in the classic *Starfleet Technical Manual* by Franz Joseph.

SNAPSHOT: The Federation Council has over and over again proven the value of a democracy in uniting many peoples from disparate backgrounds and even different planets. The Council serves as the Federation's legislature and oversees Starfleet. As bureaucracies go, it seems benign but is subject to being swayed in one direction or another by people of power or passion.

WHO'D WIN?

The Federation Council passes a resolution recognizing the Galactic Senate and welcoming it with open arms. The resolution suggests a number of ways in which the two governments might be able to work together toward common goals and lays out a suggested framework for such involvement.

The Galactic Senate struggles to pull together enough of a quorum that it can bring the Federation resolution to be read out loud on the floor and entered into the official record. Once it does, most of the senators would prefer to talk about the current problems with the Trade Federation instead.

The representatives of Starfleet sent to personally deliver the messages are made to cool their heels on Coruscant for weeks. Eventually, one of the Starfleet ensigns is accused of stealing drinks he didn't realize he had to pay for, and the resultant public outrage gathers enough attention that the Senate votes to officially reject the Federation's resolution. Several other Senate resolutions are proposed as a response, but none of them can garner enough collective support to even be brought to the floor for a final vote.

RESULT: Like it or not, the Federation Council gets things done.

THE UNDERWORLD

Not everything that happens in a galaxy is legal. Sentient creatures of all species and planetary origins have appetites and emotions that sometimes cause them to break their laws. Get enough of that together, and you have a business that the professional criminals can help you take care of.

Where there are enough people, there is crime. Where there is enough crime, there's a racket. With enough rackets, you get the kind of interstellar organization that's efficient enough to put most legitimate governments to shame.

JABBA THE HUTT VS. ZEK

JABBA THE HUTT

OCCUPATION: Crime lord, father, and lover of the finest in slave girl entertainment

DATAPOINT: Larry Ward, the actor who provided the voice of Jabba in *Star Wars: Return of the Jedi*, passed away in 1985.

SNAPSHOT: Jabba the Hutt has spent decades building up his criminal empire. There is little illegal happening on Tatooine or some of its nearby planets that he doesn't have his massive, slimy tail in. Still, Jabba is a creature driven by his emotions, his appetites, and his need to ensure that no one ever feels they can jack him around. He kills a lot of people to make sure that message gets out, and his handsome wall display of Han Solo frozen in carbonite has become his favorite decoration for that exact reason.

ZEK

OCCUPATION: Grand Nagus of the Ferengi Alliance

DATAPOINT: Before playing Zek in *Star Trek: Deep Space Nine*, actor Wallace Shawn ate his most famous meal in *My Dinner with Andre*.

SNAPSHOT: As the leader of the Ferengi Alliance, Zek possesses one of the most devious minds in his galaxy. While he's not above breaking the law, he would never consider breaking a contract—though he might creatively interpret it to the very last letter. He may sometimes seem like a withered old fool, but the fact that he has managed to remain in charge of so many greedy Ferengi for so long is a testimony to his cunning.

WHO'D WIN?

Having heard there's contraband for sale, Zek beams down inside of Jabba's palace, surprising Jabba in the middle of chortling over Han Solo's fate. The Gamorrean guards move to intercept the Ferengi, but before they can do so, Zek produces several bars of gold-pressed latinum from his pockets and scatters them at Jabba's feet. The Gamorreans skid to a halt at a word from Jabba, and Bib Fortuna scrambles forward to gather up the precious bars before they fall into the Rancor pit.

"That's just a taste of the riches that can be yours," Zek says. "I'm here to open up this part of your galaxy to *real* business, and I want you to be a part of it."

Bib Fortuna listens to Jabba and says, "The great and powerful Jabba asks, 'What's the catch?'"

"No catch at all," says Zek. "I just want to buy your business. I'm willing to pay top prices for all of it. Everything!"

"Does 'everything' include . . . that?" Bib Fortuna says, pointing at the frozen Solo.

"Of course!" Zek says with a smile.

Jabba scowls and signals for Zek to be dropped into the Rancor pit. The Grand Nagus falls away but then beams back in front of Jabba a moment later.

"All right," he says, "I can see you're a tough negotiator. Let's try that again."

RESULT: Tie. These two could go at it this way forever.

THE GODLIKE

Sometimes the most powerful characters around aren't that way because they know people, or they're good at their jobs, or they've amassed a great deal of political capital, or they're just swell folks. Sometimes it's because they have the power of gods.

Of course, if power corrupts, then the power of a god is going to play water polo with your head. People who have no limits on what they can do—other than what they themselves impose—often decide it's not worth it to bother with what other people think about them. That's when they become truly dangerous.

EMPEROR PALPATINE VS. Q

EMPEROR PALPATINE

OCCUPATION: Ruler of the Galactic Empire, Sith Lord

DATAPOINT: Emperor Palpatine was first revealed in hologram form in *Star Wars: The Empire Strikes Back.*

SNAPSHOT: Palpatine did some horrible things to become Emperor, and he's prepared to do even worse to maintain that position. While his use of the Dark Side of the Force has disfigured his body, he's stronger than ever, certainly more powerful than Darth Vader. He may, in fact, be the most powerful Master of the Force who ever lived.

Q

OCCUPATION: All-powerful being and gadfly

DATAPOINT: Q began his flirtation with humanity in "Encounter at Farpoint," the pilot episode of *Star Trek: The Next Generation.*

SNAPSHOT: As a member of the Q Continuum, Q is a being of nearly unlimited power. Despite this, he has a fondness for humanity and often intervenes to test, inspire, and even help people, though rarely in a straightforward way. He has even managed to father a child with a female Q, proving that even Q have things they can learn and ways in which they can grow.

WHO'D WIN?

"Kneel before me," Palpatine sneers at the odd man dressed in a stormtrooper's armor. "Kneel before your master."

"If I happen to see him, I'll do just that," Q says. "Meanwhile, perhaps you can offer me a reason why we should continue to permit this squalid little corner of the universe to exist. You people here really have mucked it up."

"Silence!" Palpatine commands, standing from his throne. The Sith Lord brings up his hands before him and gives Q an evil smile. "You *will* kneel before me—or you will die."

Q arches an eyebrow at the Emperor. "You really are quite full of yourself, aren't you?"

Force lightning arcs out at Q from the Emperor's fingertips. Rather than cringe in pain and terror, though, Q just shrugs. "I suppose that's meant to be painful, right? How cute."

The Emperor staggers back into his throne. "Impossible," he gasps. "You're . . . impossible!"

"Why, thank you," Q says with a smile. "You know, a lot of people say that. Now could you please move? I believe you're in my chair."

RESULT: Not even close. Q by a dozen parsecs.

OUR RUNNING TALLY

Powers

	SAGA THIS CHAPTER	RUNNING TALLY
Star Wars	1	14
Star Trek	3	13
Ties	1	3

Star Trek pounded Star Wars on this one. It has many more cosmic and all-powerful villains, like Q, after all. This brings it up to a 1-point contest again.

What kind of monster would you prefer to be eaten by? Quite possibly, the answer is "None," but in case you're wondering what it would be like, here's a quiz to test your awareness of the monsters of Star Wars and Star Trek.

1. **Supposedly if you were swallowed by a sarlacc, how long would it take for you to die?**
   A. Instant death
   B. 24 hours
   C. A week
   D. 1,000 years

2. **On the planet Neural, the horned, white ape with poisonous fangs was called a:**
   A. Mugato
   B. Snowrilla
   C. Albinape
   D. Gorn

3. **The energy-sucking creatures that lived inside the giant space slug that nearly swallowed the *Millennium Falcon* were called:**
   A. Wampas
   B. Banthas
   C. Mynocks
   D. Howlers

4. **In *Star Trek* (2009), Kirk escapes both a snow beast (a drakoulias) and a giant crablike creature (a hengrauggi) while marooned on the planet:**
   A. Vulcan
   B. Delta Vega
   C. Hoth
   D. Romulus

5. **Padmé Amidala, Obi-Wan Kenobi, and Anakin Skywalker were sent into an arena to be killed by a nexu, an acklay, and a reek, respectively, when they were captured on the planet:**
   A. Geonosis
   B. Dantooine
   C. Vendaxa
   D. Kamino

6. **The larva of the Ceti eel makes its victims susceptible to mind control by wrapping itself around a victim's brain stem after entering through the victim's:**
   A. Mouth
   B. Nose
   C. Blood
   D. Ear

Answers: 1. D, 2. A, 3. C, 4. B, 5. A, 6. D

CHAPTER 7

MONSTERS
They Live in the Shadows

Not everyone in Star Wars or Star Trek is a fully realized character with an intriguing past and ambitions for the future. Sometimes they're just creatures who want to rip things to pieces and then eat them. Or maybe forget all that chewing stuff and just swallow you whole.

Okay, they're not people. They're monsters. They may not help you examine the human condition, but they do a fantastic job at ramping up the tension.

THE BIG CRITTERS

The monsters that make the biggest first impression on you are, well, the biggest monsters. We're talking creatures the size of houses, big bloody beasties with more teeth than brain cells. They could swallow you whole and never even notice you screaming on the way down.

They're no fun at parties—or anywhere else, either.

RANCOR VS. HENGRAUGGI

RANCOR

OCCUPATION: Monster, killing machine

DATAPOINT: The rancor that first appeared in *Star Wars: Return of the Jedi* was actually an eighteen-inch-tall puppet designed by Phil Tippett.

SNAPSHOT: The fifteen-foot-tall rancor at Jabba's palace is a long way from his home on Dathomir, but life here isn't all that bad. Back home, he had to compete with other rancor for food, and there was always the chance that a couple of them might gang up to take him down and feast on his liver. Here, he has a keeper who treats him like a king, and Jabba becomes displeased with people often enough to keep him well fed. And the people who wind up down here with him aren't even tough enough to scratch his thick hide much less have him worry about breaking a tooth on them.

HENGRAUGGI

OCCUPATION: Sea monster, devourer of everything

DATAPOINT: This one is found under the ice in *Star Trek (2009)*, thanks to "creature guru" Neville Page.

SNAPSHOT: The hengrauggi is a massive monster with four legs and two arms, each of which ends in nasty, stabby claws. It also has a whiplike tongue it can use to grab its prey and haul it into its triangular maw. It's big enough to swallow you and the horse you rode in on, and not even need to floss its teeth afterward. It lives in the icy waters of Delta Vega, and it likes to lay in wait beneath the ice before breaking through it from below to snatch its prey and haul it back into the freezing waters below.

WHO'D WIN?

To settle a bet, Quark arranges to beam a rancor down onto Delta Vega. The reptilian creature immediately starts to freeze, so it stomps around the ice, hunting for shelter or at least some warm blood in which it can bathe. As the rancor clomps across the snow, a hengrauggi detects it from below and rams its way up through the ice in an attempt to swallow the rancor whole.

The hengrauggi, though, expects a smaller, less dangerous meal. It bursts out of the ice and lashes out with its tongue, which wraps around the rancor and starts hauling it in. When the rancor manages to dig its heels into the ice, though, it stops the hengrauggi from hauling it under. For a moment, the two beasts engage in a tug of war that ends only when the rancor rips the hengrauggi's ropelike tongue straight out of its mouth.

Enraged, the hengrauggi attacks the rancor again, this time trying to swallow the beast whole. The rancor stands its ground and roars up at the hengrauggi, doing its best to tell the beast that the rancor will not make for an easy meal. The hengrauggi ignores this, internally thanks the rancor for standing still while screaming, and smashes down mouth-first to engulf the rancor.

RESULT: The hengrauggi thinks the rancor is tasty and would like more.

UNDERGROUND BEASTS

Monsters that live underground serve to remind us that one of the things that should serve as the bedrock of our lives—the ground beneath our feet—really isn't stable at all. At any point, the earth could open up beneath you, and you and whatever building you're standing next to could disappear into it forever.

The underground world is so different from our own, it should be no surprise that the monsters that live there can be much different, too. They're often blind, having no need to see in eternal darkness, and they usually find their food in ways that don't make a lot of sense to those of us who live in daylight and wide-open spaces.

SARLACC VS. HORTA

SARLACC

OCCUPATION: Living means of execution

DATAPOINT: This beast makes a brief cameo in the video game *Star Wars: Jedi Knight: Jedi Academy.*

SNAPSHOT: The sarlacc is a massive, ancient creature that lives beneath the sands of Tatooine. Normally only its mouth—a massive maw lined with concentric circles of savage teeth—shows through the sands in which the rest of its body remains buried. Any creature that happens to fall—or be pushed—into its mouth can anticipate a long, horrible fate, as the sarlacc's digestive juices not only cause horrible pain but work to keep the victim alive for as long as possible, in some cases up to a thousand years.

HORTA

OCCUPATION: Silicon-based life form, nanny

DATAPOINT: The horta appeared in *Star Trek: The Original Series* episode "The Devil in the Dark," when it menaced a group of miners who were destroying its eggs.

SNAPSHOT: A horta is a creature made out of living rock. It secretes a powerful acid it can use to tunnel straight through the hardest rock. Unable to communicate directly, it can makes its thoughts known via Vulcan mind meld. The horta just wants to be left alone to care for its long-gestating offspring, but if someone tries to damage its eggs, it reacts with swift, acidic force.

WHO'D WIN?

To see if he can rid Jabba of one of his favorite cruelties, Luke Skywalker transports a horta to Tatooine and drops it onto the sand next to the sarlacc's massive throat. The sarlacc feels the disruption in the sand above it and starts questing around with its tongue, but the canny horta avoids this by tunneling underground straight away.

At this point, the sarlacc is doomed. It's normally well protected from any attack from above. All it has to do is close its mouth to prevent itself from being hurt. The horta, though, can attack it not from the top but from its sides, and it proceeds to tunnel through the sand and rock surrounding the sarlacc and do just that.

It doesn't take long for the horta to burn its way straight through the sarlacc's side and wind up in the immobile creature's gullet. And since the horta is immune to even the sarlacc's unique stomach acid, that doesn't present a problem.

It just means the horta can kill the sarlacc faster.

RESULT: The sarlacc finds out the hard way that not being able to move can make survival tricky. The horta kills it and eats its corpse.

SNOW BEASTS

It's bad enough when you're stomping around an ice planet that you already have to worry about frostbite, hypothermia, and freezing your butt off. To make matters worse, you may not be alone. The kinds of predators that can survive in such a harsh environment are just the sort of hard-asses that can make your life short, miserable, or some combination of the two.

At least you might finally be warm again inside the creature's belly. You just won't be alive to enjoy it.

WAMPA VS. DRAKOULIAS

WAMPA

OCCUPATION: Snowbound predator

DATAPOINT: Actor Des Webb wore the wampa suit for *Star Wars: The Empire Strikes Back.*

SNAPSHOT: Wampa live in the frozen wastes of the ice planet Hoth, where they rule supreme. Massive creatures with vicious claws, their pristine white fur helps them blend into their environment so well it's hard for anyone who might stumble across one to actually distinguish it from the surrounding snow. Wampas like to eat their meals fresh, so they often take extra food home to hang in their caves until they're ready to tear the cooling corpse down and indulge in a feast.

DRAKOULIAS

OCCUPATION: Predator, prey

DATAPOINT: The drakoulias appeared on Delta Vega in *Star Trek (2009)*.

SNAPSHOT: The drakoulias is also known as a polarilla, as it resembles a cross between a polar bear and a gorilla. It sprints after its prey on four powerful legs, and it brings it down with its saberlike fangs. The drakoulias prefers to take down its prey fast and then drag it off to a safe place to devour it. Otherwise, it's too easy to fall prey to the larger predators swimming beneath the ice.

WHO'D WIN?

Dropped onto Delta Vega after nearly destroying the starship that was hauling him off to an interplanetary zoo, the wampa feels right at home in the icy wastes of this alien planet—right up until a drakoulias decides to welcome him to the planet in its own horrible way. The animal bursts out of the snow in which it has been lying hidden, conserving heat and waiting for a victim to wander by.

The wampa spins, stands up on its hind legs, and squares off against the drakoulias. The two beasts clash in a horrifying clatter of teeth and claws punctuated by terrifying snarls of rage and heartbreaking howls of pain.

In the end, the smarter, larger wampa carries the day by disemboweling the drakoulias with its vicious claws. Bloodied but alive, the wampa also has the presence of mind to throw the drakoulias's corpse at a hengrauggi that appears just then, hoping to distract it for a moment while the wampa can race away.

RESULT: The wampa survives at least its first day on Delta Vega.

HORNY BEASTS

There's one sort of natural weaponry that stands out among monsters. They all have teeth, the better to devour you with. And most of them have claws, the better to tear you apart with. Few of them, though, have massive horns, the better to stab straight through you with.

REEK VS. MUGATO

REEK

OCCUPATION: Beast of burden, arena entertainment

DATAPOINT: It stomps its way into the Star Wars universe in the movie *Star Wars: Attack of the Clones.*

SNAPSHOT: The gigantic reeks hail from the planet Ylesia, where they roam free and sometimes serve as beasts of burden. A rare few of them have been trained to be the sort of aggressive brutes that do well in arena battles, and in this role they make frightening combatants. They're not naturally aggressive, but when pushed beyond reason, they can use any of the three massive horns on their head to ruin your whole day.

MUGATO

OCCUPATION: Crazed man-eating primate

DATAPOINT: A mugato poisons Kirk in the season-two episode of *Star Trek: The Original Series* called "A Private Little War."

SNAPSHOT: The mugato is a top-level predator from the planet Neural, which only recently saw the native people get their hands on primitive firearms. Its white fur makes it stand out against the foliage in its environment, which is usually enough to warn others away. It resembles a great ape with a tall, thick horn spiking out of the top of its head. Its most lethal attack, though, comes from the venom it injects into a victim through its jagged teeth.

WHO'D WIN?

One on one, a mugato wouldn't stand a chance against a reek. The reek is much larger than the mugato, and the reek's thick hide would provide protection from the mugato's venom. The arena masters of Geonosis recognize this too, so they throw three mugatos against a single reek in an arena combat to the death.

The mugatos come storming out of their cage and into the arena where they find the irritated reek already waiting for them. Dropping their horns, the mugato charge straight at the reek, hoping to impale it on their horns.

If nothing else, the reek knows how to deal with creatures with horns. It lowers its own head and meets the mugatos' charge. Two of the creatures escape, but the reek impales the third on its center horn and tosses its already lifeless corpse high into the air.

The surviving mugatos latch onto the reek and try to bite it, but their teeth aren't long enough to do more than scratch the reek's hide. But it still kinda hurts, so the reek drops to its knees and rolls to the left and then the right, crushing the surviving mugato under its fantastic bulk.

RESULT: It's going to take a lot more mugatos than that to take out a reek.

GIANT SPACE BEASTS

You blast off or beam away from a planet to the safety of wide-open space, and you figure you've got nothing to worry about but Klingon patrols or perhaps the occasional Imperial entanglement. Instead, you discover there's something else out there with you, something lurking in the darkest bits between the stars.

And it's hungry.

SPACE SLUG VS. SPACE AMOEBA

SPACE SLUG

OCCUPATION: Feeding on asteroids and the passing ship

DATAPOINT: The slug almost takes a bite out of the *Falcon* in *Star Wars: The Empire Strikes Back.*

SNAPSHOT: The space slug is a gigantic creature capable of swallowing a spaceship whole. It lives inside an airless asteroid, which it burrows through, feeding on the frozen rock. It's rare for a space slug to eat anything other than rock, but if you're desperate and careless enough to hide inside an asteroid while you're on the run, you might find that the cave you've taken refuge inside isn't really a cave after all.

SPACE AMOEBA

OCCUPATION: Gigantic virus infecting the galaxy

DATAPOINT: This creature appears in "The Immunity Syndrome," episode 47 of *Star Trek: The Original Series.*

SNAPSHOT: The space amoeba wanders through space until it finds energy it can feed on and siphon away. It managed to kill every living thing in star system Gamma 7A in Sector 39J, including those aboard the Vulcan starship *Intrepid.* It's not evil, though, just hungry. Who could fault it for wanting to feed itself?

WHO'D WIN?

The space amoeba moves into the asteroid belt outside of Hoth, and the space slug starts to feel sluggish. Despite its strange biology that allows it to thrive alone and unprotected in outer space, the space slug is still a living creature, and it cannot continue to live without the energy the space amoeba is draining from everything in the system.

Concerned, the space slug moves out of the cave it carved into its asteroid, and it squints up at the glowing mass moving toward it as it makes its way deeper into the system. It cannot appreciate the creature's colorful form, but it knows that it doesn't want it to come any closer.

Within minutes, the space amoeba engulfs the portion of the asteroid belt in which the space slug lies. As large as the slug might be, the amoeba dwarfs it, and the slug is digested soon after it enters the amoeba's mass.

The amoeba then turns toward the distant ice planet, hoping that it will make for more of a meal than one little space slug.

RESULT: Sadly, space slugs cannot generate antimatter.

OUR RUNNING TALLY

Monsters

	SAGA THIS CHAPTER	RUNNING TALLY
Star Wars	2	16
Star Trek	3	16
Ties	0	3

Star Trek gains only a small edge here, but it's enough to tie the competition up. Both franchises have plenty of fantastic monsters in them. It's just that Star Trek has so many more.

QUIZ 8

Whether it's a hapless Red Shirt from the *Enterprise* or Jar-Jar-Can-My-Accent-Get-Any-Cheesier-Binks, some characters are just, well, losers. How well do you know them?

1. **By the time of *Star Wars: Attack of the Clones*, Jar-Jar Binks has been made:**
   A. Redundant
   B. Into a villain
   C. A senator from Naboo
   D. Angry—you wouldn't like him when he's angry

2. **Wesley Crusher left Starfleet and the *Enterprise* behind to wander the galaxy with:**
   A. Beverly Crusher
   B. Thomas Riker
   C. Locutus of Borg
   D. The Traveler

3. **Lando Calrissian somehow managed to put himself in charge of Cloud City on the planet:**
   A. Hoth
   B. Endor
   C. Coruscant
   D. Bespin

4. **Quark's younger brother Rom eventually became:**
   A. The commander of Deep Space Nine
   B. The Grand Nagus of the Ferengi
   C. A Dominion spy
   D. The first Ferengi admitted to Starfleet Academy

5. **In the podrace in which Anakin Skywalker won his freedom, his owner Watto placed a huge bet on:**
   A. Anakin
   B. Jar-Jar Binks
   C. Sebulba
   D. Gardulla

6. **The Klingon solution to the troubles that tribbles gave them was to:**
   A. Destroy the tribbles' home planet
   B. Make tribble soup
   C. Put tribbles on their menus
   D. Turn tribbles into pets

Answers: 1. C, 2. D, 3. D, 4. B, 5. C, 6. A

CHAPTER 8

LOSERS
Because Not Everyone
Can Be a Winner

Some people just can't win. You can be competent and charismatic, even when you're fighting on the wrong side. But this chapter is about the losers of both universes, characters who just can't seem to catch a break, the ones for whom everything always seems to go wrong. And the characters the haters love to hate.

HAPLESS HEROES

Even the good guys have their share of losers. These are the wannabes who come along for the ride and then prove themselves to be far more trouble than they're worth. With luck, they wind up contributing in some way to the heroes' victory. In fact, their efforts may make the difference between life and death. If only they were just easier to be around the rest of the time.

JAR-JAR BINKS VS. WESLEY CRUSHER

JAR-JAR BINKS

OCCUPATION: Gungan outcast, Jedi guide

DATAPOINT: Jar-Jar was many fans' least favorite part of *Star Wars: The Phantom Menace.*

SNAPSHOT: Jar-Jar hasn't done a lot of good in his life, unless you count the good amount of damage he's inflicted on his people. It's not that he wants to hurt anyone. It's the opposite of that really. But accidents seem to stalk him like Boba Fett. Even though he's been banished from his hometown of Otoh Gunga, Jar-Jar remains optimistic that things will work out. He just wishes he knew how to help.

WESLEY CRUSHER

OCCUPATION: Starfleet ensign, Warp field prodigy

DATAPOINT: Wesley's last appearance in *Star Trek: The Next Generation* came in the episode "Journey's End."

SNAPSHOT: Wesley Crusher is a genius-level kid who's finding it hard to live up to the promise of his abilities. Part of this may extend from the fact that he spent most of his life on a starship, associating with people much older than him, and he often feels as though he doesn't really fit in anywhere. To his dismay, his time at Starfleet Academy didn't seem to be going the way he'd hoped either, and he started to question whether he really wants to be a part of Starfleet at all. Because of that, he set off with the Traveler to learn more about the galaxy and maybe even find himself.

WHO'D WIN?

While wandering with the Traveler, Crusher arrives on Naboo and relaxes on a picturesque shore. Jar-Jar spots him there and believes the strange human to be a Separatist spy, so he tries to sneak up on him and take him out. As he creeps up on Wesley, though, Jar-Jar trips, falls, and somersaults right past him to wind up in the water.

Laughing, Wesley gives Jar-Jar a hand up out of the water, surprising the Gungan with his friendliness.

"It's okay," Wesley says. "I'm not going to hurt you. But . . . ?" He hesitates until Jar-Jar's eyestalks rise in anticipation. "Do you know anywhere I could get some decent food around here?"

"Of corbse! Meesa know just where ta bring yous!" The two walk off toward drier land, in the direction of Theed. "But tell meesa this. Why you so nice to meesa?"

Wesley smiles. "I've learned a lot of things in my travels, but there's one simple rule I try to always live by."

"What that be?"

"Don't be a dick."

RESULT: Wesley kills him with kindness.

GREEDY GOOFS

When you don't have much in the way of brains, life seems easier if you just concentrate on the simple things—like doing whatever you can to earn fast and easy money. And it doesn't matter if you have to do the wrong thing to earn it. The fast and easy part trumps the right and wrong part any day, at least for these losers who'd sell out their own mothers if the price was right.

And it wouldn't take much for them to think it was right.

GREEDO VS. ROM

GREEDO

OCCUPATION: Bounty hunter

DATAPOINT: Greedo did not shoot first in *Star Wars: A New Hope*.

SNAPSHOT: Greedo's always been a bad seed. He knew Anakin Skywalker in his youth, but back then the Rodian had been a whiny, grasping brat. He hasn't improved much over the years. Not having any skills to trade on, Greedo does small jobs for Jabba the Hutt. At the moment, he's on the hunt for the smuggler Han Solo, hoping to collect the price on his head—or take a bribe from Solo to look the other way.

ROM

OCCUPATION: Waiter at Quark's Bar

DATAPOINT: Rom, along with his son Nog and his older brother Quark, visits Roswell, New Mexico, in the *Star Trek: Deep Space Nine* episode "Little Green Men."

SNAPSHOT: Rom has trailed Quark in smarts, looks, and—most important—money his entire life, and he's getting tired of it. Rom lost his savings and his love when he allowed his father-in-law to rip him off over an extension of his marriage contract, and now he's stuck on Deep Space Nine, working for Quark. There's only so much abuse a Ferengi can take, even if he's not very good at being a Ferengi.

WHO'D WIN?

Greedo strolls into Quark's Bar, looking for Han Solo. He hasn't been able to find the smuggler anywhere, but he figures he might have a chance in a place like this. After scoping the place out, he realizes he's struck out again, so he sits down at a corner table by himself and starts to get drunk.

An hour later, Greedo is three sheets to the sarlacc, and all out of gold-pressed latinum. Quark orders Rom to get rid of the Rodian, who's taking up space Quark needs for paying customers. Grumbling, Rom goes over and nudges Greedo with his serving tray, and the galaxy's worst bounty hunter goes for his gun and shoots Rom right in the chest.

Fortunately, Greedo is seeing two Roms at the moment, and he picks the wrong one. The shot goes wide, and Rom clobbers Greedo over the head with his serving tray until the Rodian decides that maybe being unconscious right now isn't such a bad thing after all.

RESULT: Greedo gets served.

CREEPY LOSERS

Not every villain is an icon to send shivers racing up and down your entire central nervous system. Some of them are just, let's face it, lame. They try to come off as bad-asses, but instead they just seem like they're overcompensating for other disappointments in their lives. They're not fooling anyone, maybe not even themselves.

SEBULBA VS. THE GORN CAPTAIN

SEBULBA

OCCUPATION: Podracer and cheat

DATAPOINT: It's Sebulba who races against Anakin in *Star Wars: The Phantom Menace*.

SNAPSHOT: Sebulba rode his souped-up podracer from humble beginnings all the way to the top of the circuit on Tatooine. He got where he is not just by being an excellent racer but also by means of his willingness to cheat, sabotage, and even injure or kill those who stood in his way. As a Dug, he's used to the higher gravity from his home planet Malastare, so even just being on Tatooine makes him feel more powerful, feeding his dangerous arrogance.

THE GORN CAPTAIN

OCCUPATION: Starship captain and brute

DATAPOINT: The Gorn captain battles Captain Kirk in the *Star Trek: The Original Series* episode "Arena," an episode in which a faulty explosion created lifelong hearing problems for William Shatner.

SNAPSHOT: The Gorn believe the Federation have invaded their territory, and it's the captain's job to destroy a Federation colony on Cestus III. It may be a dirty job, but he relishes the chance to defend his people. He's not smart, fast, or eloquent, but he has muscles to spare, and damn it, he's a fine killer.

Or so he believes.

WHO'D WIN?

One of the engines on Sebulba's podracer breaks down while he's out putting it through its paces on the Tatooine desert. He guides it to a relatively soft landing that he manages to walk away from, and he sends out a distress signal. The creature that answers it first, though, is the Gorn captain. He's here to test himself against one of the locals to see if this planet is ripe for conquering.

Despite the fact that Sebulba gets around on his hands instead of his feet, he's still faster than the sluggish Gorn. He manages to stay out of the Gorn's reach long enough to reach his podracer's single working engine. He circles around it, keeping it between himself and the Gorn.

When the Gorn winds up standing in front of the engine, Sebulba leaps over and hits the ignition. The engine surges to life and leaps forward, smacking into the Gorn at the same time the jet-intake sucks him into its whirring blades. A messy moment later, Sebulba is shy one more engine—and one Gorn captain to go along with it.

RESULT: Sebulba grinds this one out for the win.

BAD BUSINESS

Being a hero doesn't always mean facing off against the big bad guys. Sometimes you have to deal with people who aren't evil, just greedy enough to not give a damn that you're out there trying to save the universe, even if the universe includes their sorry butts. Give them this, though, they may not be philanthropists, but they treat everyone equally: like sheep to be fleeced at every opportunity.

WATTO VS. QUARK

WATTO

OCCUPATION: Junk dealer, slave owner, and gambler

DATAPOINT: The CGI Watto was voiced by actor Andrew Secombe in *Star Wars: The Phantom Menace.*

SNAPSHOT: Watto is a scummy Toydarian who clawed his way to the top of the junk heap in Mos Espa and then realized he could make a living by selling that junk heap out from under himself. He's willing to trade in just about anything, people (like his slaves, Anakin and Shmi Skywalker) included. His great weakness is gambling on podracing, which thrills him to no end.

QUARK

OCCUPATION: Proprietor of the only bar on Deep Space Nine

DATAPOINT: Part of the core ensemble of *Star Trek: Deep Space Nine,* Quark also appeared in an episode of *Star Trek: The Next Generation* and in the pilot episode of *Star Trek: Voyager.*

SNAPSHOT: Quark is the Ferengi's Ferengi. He lives by the Rules of Acquisition and can quote it chapter and verse to help rationalize his most important decisions. He had thought he had a good thing going, running the only bar on the Cardassian space station Terok Nor, and when the Cardassians left he had planned on joining them—until Captain Sisko made him an offer to stay that he couldn't afford to refuse. Quark always has his eyes peeled for the next big deal, but he never—okay, rarely—allows that to pull him away from making sure his bar always turns a profit.

WHO'D WIN?

On a junk-finding tour of other parts of the galaxy, Watto stops at Deep Space Nine for an overnight stay and decides to check out the action at the local watering hole. While there, Quark takes the winged stranger under his arm and teaches him how to play one of the most popular games of chance in all of Feringar: Dabo.

After a few rounds of play, Watto has doubled his stake and is feeling good. That's when the Dabo girls start paying a lot more attention to him, trying to distract him from the game. Watto sees right through the ploy though. Figuring that he's figured out Quark's real game and spotted himself an unbeatable edge, he puts everything he has on the table for one last spin of the wheel.

To Watto's disbelief, the wheel comes up empty for him, and the Dabo girl sweeps all of his gold-pressed latinum off the table. Enraged, he turns on Quark, but Odo, chief of security on the station, puts a quick stop to that.

RESULT: Watto leaves Quark's with his pockets far lighter than when he entered. Give this one to the Ferengi.

LITTLE PESTS

Even the darkest stories have their lighter moments, which serve to put the blacker bits in higher contrast and make us appreciate them all the more for it. Of course, the characters that appear in these lighter moments are hardly the stuff of which epics are fashioned. Instead, they often appear to be pests, especially at first, even if they turn out to be vital components of the story as it races headlong toward its endgame.

WICKET W. WARWICK VS. TRIBBLES

WICKET W. WARWICK

OCCUPATION: Hero of the Ewoks

DATAPOINT: A short mockumentary about actor Warwick Davis's fictional transformation into Wicket was made as a promotion for *Star Wars: Return of the Jedi* but never released. To date, the full film has only ever been screened at official Star Wars conventions.

SNAPSHOT: Wicket W. Warrick is already a hero of his people before the Rebels arrive. He's displayed his bravery dozens of times by scouting the base the Empire installed on Endor, which generates the force field that served to protect the Death Star II while it was under construction. While most Ewoks were content to remain hidden in the forest and let the bigger peoples wage war on each other, Warrick's curiosity drove him to learn more about the situation to ensure that his people would not be caught unawares.

TRIBBLES

OCCUPATION: Terminally cute pets/pests

DATAPOINT: They started breeding in the *Star Trek: The Original Series* episode "The Trouble With Tribbles" and continued on Deep Space Nine in "Trials and Tribble-ations."

SNAPSHOT: Tribbles like to eat and breed and max out the cute enough so that no one gets tempted to kill them. Rabbits get tired thinking about how fast tribbles reproduce. Each of them can have up to ten offspring every twelve hours, which means they can overwhelm any area without predators in short order. They don't much care, though. They just keep making more tribbles.

WHO'D WIN?

A young Zek purchases a tribble from a smuggler, figuring that it can't be hard to turn a profit on a creature that multiplies so fast. When he realizes his error, he kills the tribbles and beams their remains down to the surface of a nearby moon called Endor to get rid of them. One of the dying tribbles manages to reproduce before it finally expires, and that one healthy litter of tribbles begins to create more and more tribbles in the planet's massive forest.

Wicket W. Warrick discovers one of the creatures and decides to bring it back to the Ewok village to show to his friends and family. It's not long before the place is overrun with tribbles, and the Ewoks begin hunting the creatures to get rid of them. But it's Warrick that makes the discovery that encourages every Ewok on the moon to chip in and help out with the effort.

It turns out that—to an Ewok, at least—tribbles are delicious.

RESULT: Warrick makes a meal out of the tribbles—and comes back for seconds and thirds.

OUR RUNNING TALLY

Losers

	SAGA THIS CHAPTER	RUNNING TALLY
Star Wars	2	18
Star Trek	3	19
Ties	0	3

By having the better losers, Star Trek edges out Star Wars in this category and grabs its first lead. Having better losers may be damning yourself with faint praise, but it if means taking the lead, so be it.

PART II

GADGETS

Think you know all there is to know about the advanced technology of Star Wars and Star Trek?

1. **The name of Obi-Wan's droid destroyed during the Battle of Coruscant in *Star Wars: Revenge of the Sith* is:**
   A. R4-G9
   B. R2-D2
   C. WA-7
   D. R4-P17

2. **The tablet computer interfaces used by Starfleet in *The Next Generation* are called:**
   A. PADDs
   B. WINs
   C. SLAYTs
   D. JERNULLs

3. **R2-D2 is what kind of droid?**
   A. Astromech
   B. Protocol
   C. Battle
   D. Construction

4. **Transporting in *Star Trek* is often called:**
   A. Shining
   B. Snatching
   C. Zapping
   D. Beaming

5. **Which *Star Wars* character made a very short appearance in *Star Trek* (2009)?**
   A. Yoda
   B. R2-D2
   C. A wampa
   D. C-3PO

6. **The android Data had a twin named:**
   A. Lore
   B. Datta
   C. Byte
   D. Myth

CHAPTER 9

TECHNOLOGY
Futuristic Gadgets
From Our Past

The whiz-bang part of any science fiction story is the science, or at least the pseudo-science that passes for it. There's nothing quite like a world with (an)droids running all over the place, advising you on how to best navigate using your preferred faster-than-light drive or about which of the polarities of the various available made-up subatomic particles you might want to flip-flop. Star Wars, of course, heaps in a healthy dose of mysticism with its fake science, but no one gives better techno babble than an episode of Star Trek. Let's bash these bits against each other to see which survive.

THE (AN)DROIDS

Artificial life forms play a huge role in both universes. Star Wars is filthy with droids. The creatures handle almost every menial task and many that require advanced combinatorial mathematics too. Star Trek, on the other hand, features only a handful of androids, though if you want to you could lump them in with the artificial intelligences that help run Starfleet's ships. So let's figure out which is better!

C-3PO VS. DATA

C-3PO

OCCUPATION: Human-cyborg relations

DATAPOINT: One of the most iconic elements of the original *Star Wars: A New Hope*, C-3PO was originally built by Anakin Skywalker.

SNAPSHOT: C-3PO may specialize in the translation of countless different languages, making sure that people and machines across the galaxy can talk to each other, but the amazing part about him is his knack for getting out of all the tight situations in which he often seems to find himself. For all the adventures he's had with R2-D2, though, he doesn't seem to appreciate a single one of them. If he had his choice, he'd prefer to work at a quiet, stable job for the rest of his mechanical life.

DATA

OCCUPATION: Operations officer aboard the *Enterprise*

DATAPOINT: One of Star Trek's most enduring characters, beginning with the pilot episode of *Star Trek: The Next Generation*, Data is a lieutenant commander who attended Starfleet Academy 2341–45.

SNAPSHOT: Data has learned a lot since he was first assigned to the *Enterprise*. Though he still hasn't managed to master emotions, he has come to understand human concepts like friendship and love and how to respect them, even if he can't personally experience them. While Data is potentially the smartest creature that ever served with Starfleet, he is still a child in many senses, innocent of the ways of the world but forging his way through it in any case.

WHO'D WIN?

Data beams down to Mos Eisley in search of a supply of dilithium, which his tricorder detects in the back room of the Cantina

Bar. After being told they don't serve his kind here, he winds up cooling his heels outside, where he meets C-3PO. When Data asks C-3PO if he knows a back way into the Cantina, C-3PO starts to get nervous, and he gets even more jittery when a patrol of stormtroopers roams by.

"You seem to have an advanced emotional subroutine installed," Data says. "Fascinating."

"Not really," said C-3PO. "It's standard in all droids. It's what allows us to put matters into a sentient context so that we can known how to relate better to our masters."

"You are slaves?"

"I am a protocol droid, fluent in over six million forms of communication, and this is my counterpart, R2-D2. We belong to Master Luke now."

"Fluent in six million forms of communication?" Data replies. "So is my universal translator. I could not help but notice you grew agitated when local law enforcement passed by."

"Oh, dear," C-3PO says. "Master Luke would prefer to avoid any Imperial entanglements."

And that's when another stormtrooper appears as if from nowhere. "Hey, you three," he barks at the waiting droids. "Let's see your registrations."

"Oh, dear," C-3PO gasps.

"I have my registration materials right here, my good sir," Data responds, pulling his phaser instead. He quickly stuns the stormtrooper.

"Oh, dear, oh, dear," C-3PO all but weeps.

"Now," Data says to the agitated protocol droid, "please ask your little friend to help me unlock the back door to the Cantina. Lieutenant Commander LaForge is waiting for that dilithium."

RESULT: Data keeps his cool, and he proves himself to be the superior AI.

THE NAVIGATORS

When you're trying to make your way from one side of the galaxy to another, it really helps if you not only have a map but also know how to use it. Otherwise, you might run your starship right through the middle of a star, or bounce too close to a supernova—that would end your trip real quick. It's not enough just to know where you are and where you're going, you also need to know the best way to get there. That's where the navigators come in.

R2-D2 VS. PAVEL CHEKOV

R2-D2

OCCUPATION: Astromech droid and revolutionary

DATAPOINT: His name may derive from an incident when George Lucas overheard a sound editor ask for Reel 2, Dialogue Track 2 of *American Graffiti*, abbreviated as R-2-D-2.

SNAPSHOT: R2-D2 started out in the service of Queen Amidala of Naboo, but he has served many other masters over the years. For a while, he worked with Princess Leia as part of the Rebel Alliance, but he has since been assigned to help navigate Luke Skywalker's X-wing starfighter. R2 is far more than a simple navigational computer, though, having accompanied his friends through many dangerous missions and having helped defeat the Emperor and so restore freedom to the galaxy.

PAVEL CHEKOV

OCCUPATION: Starfleet navigator

DATAPOINT: Walter Koenig, who played Chekov, also appeared as bad guy Bester in *Babylon 5*.

SNAPSHOT: To become the navigator of the *Enterprise* at such a tender age was a dream come true for Pavel Chekov, and he's made the most of it. He's known to volunteer for all sorts of other duties as his time and responsibilities permit, and he's even been a part of many away teams. Chekov hopes he has a long and fruitful career aboard the *Enterprise*, as he hopes to someday captain a ship of his own.

WHO'D WIN?

Accidentally piloting the *Millennium Falcon* to an unknown part of the galaxy, R2-D2 needs more information about where he happens to be—and then it arrives in the form of the *Enterprise*. Chekov beams aboard the *Falcon* as part of an away team looking for survivors on what they believe to be a derelict ship. There he encounters R2-D2 and tries to establish communications with the little droid.

While R2 can understand Chekov just fine, the same isn't true for Chekov when R2 whistles and moans at him. When Chekov tries to pry the droid open, R2 gives the man enough of a shock to knock him flat on his back. Chekov scrambles to his feet and draws his phaser, leveling it at the droid.

"One more move like that," he says, "and I will waporize you."

With a submissive hoot, R2 plugs into the *Millennium Falcon*'s control system. Using a handy screen, R2 can finally communicate with Chekov that he's lost. Chekov is able to provide R2 with a few key waypoint stars, and then the two navigators begin to chart return courses.

"Course plotted!" Chekov announces triumphantly, but R2 whistles in response. He's already got a dozen better options plotted and is waiting for Chekov to beam off the *Falcon* so he can be on his way.

RESULT: The race goes to R2-D2, who can plug directly into the navigation computer.

THE ENGINEERS

A starship may be a wonderful machine when it leaves its dry dock and heads out into space for the first time: fast, sleek, and apparently unstoppable. Once it gets into its first scrap with an enemy ship, though, all bets are off. If that happens to you, you'd better make sure you have a talented engineer aboard. It's going to be a long way home if you have to get out and push.

ANAKIN SKYWALKER VS. MONTGOMERY "SCOTTY" SCOTT

ANAKIN SKYWALKER

OCCUPATION: Slave, mechanic, brat, podracer, Chosen One

DATAPOINT: Anakin's adventures during the Clone Wars are described in the comic series *Star Wars: Republic.*

SNAPSHOT: Anakin is a gifted kid born to the slave Shmi Skywalker, who works at Watto's Shop in Mos Espa. Practically growing up in a junkyard, he's a mechanical genius who built his own podracer out of Watto's junk just so he could become the youngest podracer on the competition's lethal circuit. And he's been working on a protocol droid of his own, too.

MONTGOMERY "SCOTTY" SCOTT

OCCUPATION: Chief engineer of the *Enterprise*

DATAPOINT: In a 1962 episode of *Bonanza,* James Doohan, who portrayed Scotty, appeared with Majel Barrett, later Nurse Chapel aboard the *Enterprise.*

SNAPSHOT: Scotty is one of the finest engineers in the Federation. He's built his reputation on underpromising and overdelivering results. He's a clever man who enjoys his own jokes even if everyone else doesn't always appreciate them, and he's a proud Scotsman who drinks scotch, plays the bagpipes, and wears a kilt for ceremonial occasions.

WHO'D WIN?

Scotty wanders into Watto's Shop as Qui-Gon Jinn attempts to negotiate with Watto over the spare parts he needs to be able to fix Queen Amidala's starship so they can get off Tatooine and continue on their way. Ani has already offered to help with the repairs, but he can't do anything without the parts from Watto, which none of them can afford.

"I'd be happy to take a look at your wee problem," Scotty says. Once Qui-Gon explains the trouble, Scotty smiles. "That's nae problem at all. I'll just fire up the replicator and have one for ye in nothing flat."

On his way out, Scotty spies Ani working on his podracer and offers to take a look at it. He can't understand how half of it manages to hang together under race conditions—Ani unwittingly holds them together with the Force—but he points out that by reversing the polarity of the turbines, Ani could gain a 50 percent power boost.

RESULT: Ani may be the Chosen One—if you're trying to choose who gets to become Darth Vader—but when it comes to engineering, he's a gifted amateur. Scotty for the win.

THE DOCTORS

When heroes suffer a setback, it often hurts worse than stubbing your toe. It involves horrible diseases, madness, or lost hands that go spiraling off into the deepest air shafts ever seen. When these horrible things happen, they need the best medical care their society can provide. Let's just hope they have their health insurance paid up so they can get it.

ZAK ZAZ VS. DR. LEONARD "BONES" MCCOY

ZAK ZAZ

OCCUPATION: Doctor in a hospital in Sundari on the planet Mandalore

DATAPOINT: He first appeared in the *Star Wars: The Clone Wars* episode "Corruption."

SNAPSHOT: Zak Zaz is a seasoned physician and scientist who's proud to be a part of the New Mandalorian movement that advocates pacifism and neutrality during the Clone Wars. His people have suffered for their wish to remain outside of the larger conflict, but he works tirelessly to alleviate as much of that as he can. Using modern means, he finds that there are few ailments he cannot help with, and when he stumbles upon a more challenging case, he dedicates himself to it the best he can.

DR. LEONARD "BONES" MCCOY

OCCUPATION: Chief medical officer of the *Enterprise*

DATAPOINT: DeForest Kelley, who portrayed Bones, spent the first part of his acting career primarily playing villains.

SNAPSHOT: Bones is a crackerjack physician who's seen—and solved—more strange cases in his time in Starfleet than most hospitals see in a decade. He's a man of strong emotions who's not afraid to express them, from happiness to frustration. Because he works on the frontier of medicine—in more ways than one—he's not afraid to come up with diagnoses and hypotheses on the fly, as he knows that the biggest enemy any doctor faces when dealing with the unknown is time.

WHO'D WIN?

Bones beams down to Mandalore as part of a medical exchange program with this newly discovered universe. He finds Zaz treating a number of school children who have all fallen ill in some sort of epidemic. Zaz believes that the children may have ingested something that poisoned them, and Bones asks if he can perform a noninvasive test on them.

After examining a few of the kids with his tricorder, Bones concludes that Zaz is correct, and he identifies the compound and an antidote. Zaz is thrilled at the progress but has no idea where they might be able to find enough of the antidote in time. Bones beams back up to the *Enterprise* and manufactures the medicine in his protein resequencer. Then he beams back down to deliver it to Zaz.

Zaz thanks Bones and asks if there's any way he can repay him for his help. "Well," Bones says, "I wouldn't mind having a closer look at this 'bacta' of yours."

RESULT: Despite their collegiality, Bones establishes himself as the superior physician.

THE DESIGNERS

When you're desperate, it's not enough to be able to maintain and repair the equipment you have. You need someone around who can come up with new devices on the fly and create items with applications that help solve problems you couldn't have foreseen even existing when you set out. That's where the designers come in: the engineers who work with bleeding-edge science to create new and vital machines on a moment's notice.

WAT TAMBOR VS. GEORDI LA FORGE

WAT TAMBOR

OCCUPATION: Foreman of the Techno Union

DATAPOINT: Tambor first appeared in the novel *Star Wars: Cloak of Deception* by James Luceno

SNAPSHOT: Being from Skako, a planet with a high atmospheric pressure, Tambor must wear a metallic pressurization suit to keep himself alive on most habitable planets. For this reason, some have mistaken him for a droid. The fact that he is in charge of the Techno Union and has supervised the construction of many facilities designed to build battle droids has only reinforced this. Tambor is ambitious and arrogant. He only cares about what value others may have to him, which he often perceives to be zero. Despite being part of the Separatist Council that launched the

Confederacy of Independent Systems, he is good at covering his tracks and makes an effort to appear politically neutral, no matter how bald-faced the lie may be.

GEORDI LA FORGE

OCCUPATION: Chief engineer of the *Enterprise*

DATAPOINT: LeVar Burton, Geordie's alter ego, is also known to television viewers as the host of *Reading Rainbow*. As well, he played the young Kunta Kinte in *Roots*.

SNAPSHOT: Blind from birth, La Forge never let that or anything else stop him. When he was five, he was fitted with a VISOR to help him see, and he has been working at using science to solve problems ever since. Despite his affliction, La Forge has a sharp and warm sense of humor that he sometimes uses to mask personal pain. He has one of the sharpest minds in the Federation and is able to concoct brilliant solutions to new problems on the fly.

WHO'D WIN?

The *Enterprise* happens upon a planet that seems to be inhabited entirely by droids building more droids, and La Forge is sent down with an away team to investigate. He soon runs into Wat Tambor, who has devastated the planet with his droid factory, something he hopes to replicate on other planets as soon as possible.

Through his VISOR, La Forge can detect and identify the frequency upon which Tambor's droids communicate with each other. He could easily jam it, but that would only mean that the droids would continue on with the orders they have, relying on their onboard systems for judgment. Instead, he decides to try reprogramming the robots over the communications frequency.

La Forge pulls out his PADD and comes up with a new set of orders for the droids nearest him. Then he uses his VISOR to transmit those orders on the correct frequency. This compels the droids to go find another droid, relay the orders, and then pull themselves to pieces. In this way, the orders propagate across the entire droid population, including those far outside of the VISOR's range. Within a matter of hours, Tambor has a disaster on his hands instead of a triumph.

RESULT: La Forge's ingenuity trumps Tambor's ruthlessness.

OUR RUNNING TALLY

Technology

	SAGA THIS CHAPTER	RUNNING TALLY
Star Wars	1	19
Star Trek	4	23
Ties	0	3

Star Trek busts open the lead in this chapter. No surprise, really, since Star Trek pays a lot more attention to the science in its fiction, whereas Star Wars is better described as a science-fantasy story. This gives Star Trek the largest lead so far.

Ready to put your lightsaber up against a phaser? Test your advanced weapons training with this quiz.

1. **The number of lightsabers General Grievous can wield at once is:**
   A. One
   B. Four
   C. Two
   D. None

2. **Phasers fire beams of:**
   A. Light
   B. Nadion particles
   C. Gamma radiation
   D. Fire

3. **As a focus for its blade, a lightsaber uses Force-imbued:**
   A. Lasers
   B. Circuits
   C. Midi-chlorians
   D. Crystals

4. **Carol Marcus designed the Genesis Device to rapidly terraform planets. Who wanted to use it as a weapon?**
   A. Khan Noonien Singh
   B. General Chang
   C. The Dominion
   D. Zefram Cochrane

5. **Blasters fire bolts of:**
   A. Nadion particles
   B. Cohesive light
   C. Gamma radiation
   D. Radiation

6. **The phasers in *Star Trek (2009)* have a rotating barrel that switches between stun and kill. They're colored:**
   A. White and black
   B. Blue and red
   C. Blue and gold
   D. Red and black

Answers: 1. B, 2. B, 3. D, 4. A, 5. B, 6. B

CHAPTER 10

WEAPONS
Keeping the Galaxy Honest

The galaxy is a dangerous place, full of people and creatures that would kill you as soon as look at you. Toss in rivalries, politics, and wars, and it's hard to imagine why you'd want to go anywhere without some sort of weapon at your side. Just as a gun beats a stick, though, some weapons are clearly superior to others, and when your life is on the line, you should be sure to take every single advantage you can get.

WARRIORS

By itself, a weapon is useless. It's the people who wield them that give them power, and the more skilled those people, the more dangerous the weapon becomes. Warriors train in the use of their chosen styles of weaponry for years, knowing that if they fail in a fight, they stand to lose far more than their honor or their dignity. It's often a matter of their lives.

BOBA FETT VS. TUVOK

BOBA FETT

OCCUPATION: Bounty hunter

DATAPOINT: Fett's first appearance in public was at the 1978 San Anselmo County Fair parade.

SNAPSHOT: As an exact clone of the legendary warrior Jango Fett—who served as the template for the entire Army of the Republic used during the Clone Wars—Boba Fett was trained from birth to become the greatest and most dangerous warrior in the galaxy. After Mace Windu killed his father, young Boba was forced to fend for himself, and he soon became a successful bounty hunter whose reputation grew with every capture. Boba cares for little besides money and his reputation, and he works hard to make the best of both.

TUVOK

OCCUPATION: Tactical officer, USS *Voyager*

DATAPOINT: Tim Russ, who played Tuvok, had previously appeared in the *Star Trek: The Next Generation* episode "Starship Mine."

SNAPSHOT: A devoted father and husband, Tuvok puts just as much drive into being an excellent Starfleet officer. While his non-Vulcan shipmates sometimes confuse him with their illogical ways, he has come to respect them if not always understand them. As tactical officer for *Voyager*, Tuvok fiercely protects the ship and the people on it, whom he sees as his charges. Having undergone the deadly Vulcan ritual of *tal'oth*, Tuvok is a skilled combatant, always ready to charge to someone's defense.

WHO'D WIN?

Darth Vader wants to know more about the people aboard the *Voyager*, and he hires Boba Fett to capture one of their bridge officers and bring him or her back alive. Fett tracks down *Voyager* above Tatooine and creates a disturbance in Mos Eisley—setting the city on fire—to lure an away team down from the ship.

Tuvok arrives with Tom Paris and Harry Kim. As they materialize, Fett shoots Kim with his EE-3 carbine rifle. Furious, Paris draws his phaser and fires at Fett, who drops behind cover. He pops up to snap up a blaster pistol shot at the charging Paris and drops him.

Fett looks around, wondering where the third person went. Tuvok appears behind him, knocks the pistol from his hand, and attempts to take him down with a Vulcan nerve pinch by grabbing Fett's neck under his helmet. Fett's armor lining protects him better than Tuvok would have expected, and Fett spins around and brings up a knee into the Vulcan's stomach.

Tuvok blocks the blow, but the rocket dart that launches out of Fett's kneepad catches him by surprise. He goes down in pain and is unconscious from the dart's drugged tip an instant later.

RESULT: Fett takes down not just Tuvok but Paris and Kim too. A smashing group win for him.

PISTOLS

The favored weapon of most characters in both the Star Wars and Star Trek sagas is the pistol. The biggest difference between the two types of weapons is that Star Wars combatants use blasters, while the Federation employs phasers. Phasers shoot nadion particle beams, while blasters fire bolts of cohesive energy. Both can be deadly, but in different ways.

COMMANDER CODY VS. B'ELANNA TORRES

COMMANDER CODY

OCCUPATION: Clone army commander under General Kenobi

DATAPOINT: He was played by Temuera Morrison, who was born on North Island, New Zealand.

SNAPSHOT: As Unit 2224, Cody had more freewill and initiative than most of his clone brothers. Because of this, he became a trusted leader in the Army of the Republic during the Clone Wars and established a friendship with his Jedi leader, Obi-Wan Kenobi. Despite this, Cody's primary loyalty is to the Galactic Republic, and he follows Chancellor Palpatine's orders in all things.

B'ELANNA TORRES

OCCUPATION: Chief engineer of *Voyager,* former Maquis revolutionary

DATAPOINT: B'Elanna's journey to Sto-Vo-Kor began in the *Star Trek: Voyager* episode "Barge of the Dead."

SNAPSHOT: Born half-human and half-Klingon, Torres struggled with her sense of identity from an early age. She joined Starfleet but left it to take up with the Maquis instead. When circumstances forced her to join the crew of *Voyager* as it was trapped in the Delta Quadrant, though, she made the most of it. A lady of high principles, Torres is quick to anger and a savage defender of her friends. Despite this, she can hold her temper when required to analyze a situation with a cold eye. B'Elanna, at the brink of death, once found herself on the journey to the Klingon warrior's afterlife, Sto-Vo-Kor.

WHO'D WIN?

Commander Cody has his orders, and those include taking down anyone who stands between him and General Grievous's headquarters on the planet Utapau. Unfortunately, B'Elanna Torres winds up in the wrong place at the wrong time, and Cody mistakes her for one of the Separatists.

"Halt!" Cody calls as he raises his blaster pistol.

Surprised, Torres ducks behind a boulder and draws her phaser. Cody fires, showering her in shards of rock.

"I don't want to fight you!" Torres says. Having gotten a good look at his armor, she decides to play it safe. She flips her phaser from stun to kill.

Cody snaps off two more shots, cracking the boulder in half. It won't provide cover for much longer. "I have my orders," he says. "They include killing you."

Torres pops up, swings her arms around, and fires her phaser at Cody. It catches him in the shoulder, and his entire form disappears in a flash of light.

"Sorry to hear that," Torres says. "Mine include staying alive."

RESULT: Torres, because a gun that can disintegrate you trumps one that can knock you dead.

LIGHTSABER VS. PHASER

While a phaser might beat out a blaster, a blaster is hardly the top personal weapon in the Star Wars universe. That honor goes to the lightsaber, "an elegant weapon for a more enlightened age." The two weapons work in entirely different ways. What happens when you pit them against each other?

KIT FISTO VS. T'POL

KIT FISTO

OCCUPATION: Jedi Master

DATAPOINT: We first meet him at the Battle of Geonosis in *Star Wars: Attack of the Clones*.

SNAPSHOT: Born on the planet Glee Anselm, the young Nautolan left for the Jedi Academy at an early age. Even among the Jedi, his large, unblinking eyes and the tentacles sweeping back from the top of his head made Kit Fisto stand out. He developed his own techniques with the lightsaber that are just as unconventional as he is, making him a fearsome fighter on any field of battle.

T'POL

OCCUPATION: First officer of *Enterprise (NX-01)*

DATAPOINT: T'Pol was the first Vulcan to serve aboard a Federation starship.

SNAPSHOT: As one of the first Vulcans to work in close proximity with humans for an extended period of time, T'Pol finds humans confusing and frustrating in their stubbornness and their reliance on instinct and emotions over logic. Despite this, she is determined to integrate herself into the *Enterprise* team, while at the same time never losing her own strong sense of identity.

She is also a crack shot with a phaser.

WHO'D WIN?

T'Pol flies a shuttle down from *Enterprise* to the planet Geonosis to see if anyone requires assistance after the skirmish that she detected happening on the surface a short while ago. While she pokes around, Kit Fisto surprises her as he searches for any members of the Separatist Council that may still be hiding near the Geonosian execution arena in which the battle was fought.

Siding with caution, T'Pol fires her phaser—which is still set on stun—at Fisto. The Jedi blocks the beam with his lightsaber. It bounces off the blade and into the sky.

Fisto charges straight at his attacker. T'Pol pulls the trigger a second time. The beam once again bounces off Fisto's emerald blade. This time, though, he shifts the angle of his blade so that it bounces back at T'Pol, and she falls to the ground, stunned.

RESULT: T'Pol learns the hard way that nothing gets past a Jedi with a ready lightsaber (except maybe another Jedi). Fisto wins.

MASTERS OF THE BLADE

In a galaxy in which you can blow up a planet or just disintegrate a foe with a single shot, something like a sword seems quaint—unless, of course, it's a three-foot length of pure energy that can cut through just about anything. Those lightsabers, they're something else entirely. And not just anyone can use one. You need to be attuned to the Force—or at least be a trained master of the blade. Otherwise, you're likely to slice yourself in half before you have a chance to take on that Sith Lord.

MACE WINDU VS. HIKARU SULU

MACE WINDU

OCCUPATION: Jedi Master

DATAPOINT: Windu's purple lightsaber was the result of a personal request by actor Samuel L. Jackson to George Lucas.

SNAPSHOT: Mace Windu has long been one of the most powerful and respected Jedi in the entire order. Despite his legendary wisdom, he has developed a blind spot when it comes to the politicians that run the Galactic Republic that he and the other Jedi strive to protect. It saddens him to see the Jedi plunged into the Clone Wars, but he is determined to ensure the Republic survives.

HIKARU SULU

OCCUPATION: Helmsman of the *Enterprise*

DATAPOINT: In the pilot episode, "Where No Man Has Gone Before," Sulu was a staff physicist and didn't become the ship's pilot until later episodes.

SNAPSHOT: Hikaru Sulu takes himself and his duties seriously, but he puts just as much effort into his fun. He worked hard to graduate at the top of his class at Starfleet Academy and earn his position at the helm of the *Enterprise*, but that didn't stop him from joining Kirk and Olson on a desperate attempt to disable Nero's space drill via a space dive. Sulu is an expert swordsman and carries a retractable sword that can extend from and disappear into its hilt at the press of a button.

WHO'D WIN?

Sulu sees Mace Windu practicing with his lightsaber outside of the Jedi Academy on Coruscant, and the sight intrigues him. He watches for a while and then approaches Windu and asks if he may give the weapon a try.

Windu smiles and says, "A lightsaber is only meant to be used by those who can feel their connection to the Force. I do not sense this within you."

Sulu pulls out his retractable sword and flicks it out to its full length with the press of a button. He assumes the dueling position. "But I do know my way around a blade."

Windu smiles. "Fair enough, but we will use the training lightsabers our younglings carry. I wouldn't want you to lose a limb."

Sulu grins as Windu tosses him an unlit blade and then ignites it. In the bluish glow, he nods at Windu, who has drawn a purple blade himself.

"Ready?" asks Windu.

"En garde," Sulu says.

The fight does not last long

RESULT: Seriously? It's Mace Windu all the way.

THE ULTIMATE WEAPON

The worst weapons in the galaxy don't just kill a single person or even mow down a whole battalion of droids at a time. They wipe out entire planets, killing everything on them. Both series have their weapons of planetary destruction, but which one is the most effective?

THE DEATH STAR VS. RED MATTER

THE DEATH STAR

OCCUPATION: Blowing up planets

DATAPOINT: At the time of its destruction, the Death Star was fully staffed with 1,161,293 people. Every one of them died—except Darth Vader.

SNAPSHOT: Known as the supreme power in the galaxy, the Death Star was built at the Emperor's behest so that he can threaten any population he wishes with instant and ultimate destruction. It houses as many people as a small planet, and it can travel between systems on its own hyperspace drive. While Darth Vader claims that the Death Star is nothing next to the Dark Side of the Force, he's never turned an entire planet into an asteroid belt using the Force, so the evidence is not in his favor.

RED MATTER

OCCUPATION: Making black holes

DATAPOINT: Red Matter was invented for J. J. Abrams's *Star Trek (2009)*. It's oddly similar to the red ball that's an essential part of the Rambaldi-invented Mueller device from the TV show *Alias*—also produced by J. J. Abrams.

SNAPSHOT: Red matter is a substance that—when properly ignited—causes the formation of a black hole. It came back with Spock from the future after Nero's presence in the past had so altered time as to create an alternate universe with its own future timeline. It can be used to destroy planets, but it seems to require the sort of heat and pressure found only in the core of a planet—or in the matter-antimatter reactor of a massive, exploding starship—to ignite it.

WHO'D WIN?

Nero's *Narada* comes out of Warp near the planet Alderaan. He's been looking for Earth and believes he's found it. He moves in toward the planet and sets up his ship's massive drill so that he can bore a hole right into the center of the planet. He's not been at it for long when a massive beam of energy erupts from what he'd until then taken to be the planet's moon. The beam tears through the planet, and it explodes, taking Nero's drill with it.

Despite all the debris, the *Narada* remains intact. Nero brings his ship about to attack the Death Star, but he sticks with his traditional weaponry, not the red matter. The only way he could use it now would be to detonate his own ship around it, and as he's yet to kill Spock, he's not prepared to sell his life that way, not even for such a triumph.

The *Narada*'s weapons do little damage to the Death Star, but enough to get its attention. As the space station turns toward his ship, Nero realizes that this is not a fight he can win. Just before the *Narada* can go to Warp, though, the Death Star fires at his ship and destroys it.

Unfortunately, this ignites the red matter aboard the *Narada*. As the black hole forms, the Death Star makes a blind leap into hyperspace, barely escaping the system intact.

RESULT: Nearly a tie, but this one goes to the Death Star.

OUR RUNNING TALLY

Weapons

	SAGA THIS CHAPTER	RUNNING TALLY
Star Wars	4	23
Star Trek	1	24
Ties	0	3

Star Wars comes right back and pummels Star Trek in this category, making it a real contest once again. Are you surprised that Star Wars would have better weapons? It's about wars, after all. It's right there in the name.

QUIZ 11

Faster-than-light starships are perhaps the strongest common element between Star Wars and Star Trek. How much do you know about the ships of the line?

1. **Han Solo won the *Millennium Falcon* in a game of sabacc with:**
   A. Lando Calrissian   C. Harry Mudd
   B. Jabba the Hutt   D. Watto

2. **The Naval Construction Contract number of the *Enterprise* in *Star Trek: The Original Series* is:**
   A. NCC-1701   C. 3263827
   B. THX 1138   D. PU-36

3. **Warp 1 is the speed of light. In *Star Trek: Voyager*, Warp 10 is:**
   A. Ten times the speed of light
   B. Infinite velocity
   C. A tenth of the speed of light
   D. A thousand times the speed of light

4. **The starship Khan Noonien Singh commanded was the:**
   A. *Endeavour*   C. *Vengeance*
   B. *Botany Bay*   D. *Alcatraz*

5. **The ship owned and flown by Boba Fett was called:**
   A. *No Disintegrations*
   B. *Slave 1*
   C. *Clone Wolf*
   D. *Argo*

6. **Starfleet's first ship capable of Warp 5 was the:**
   A. *Defiant*
   B. *Enterprise NX-01*
   C. *Titan*
   D. *Bird-of-Prey*

CHAPTER 11

STARSHIPS
The Best Way to See
the Universe

All the way from Jules Verne shooting moon capsules out of gigantic rifles, straight through the *Millennium Falcon* and the *Enterprise*, and up to the real-life Space Shuttle program, starships have fired our imaginations for decades, and they promise to do so for generations to come.

But which ones are the best in our favorite fictional universes?

THE FASTEST

One thing every starship needs is speed—especially if you're a smuggler trying to run an Imperial blockade, or if you're rushing to the rescue of a colony on the edge of the Klingon Neutral Zone. The fastest ships can get you into the action in the blink of an eye, and they can move you right back out of it if things don't go your way, but only the best pilots can handle that kind of speed.

MILLENNIUM FALCON VS. VOYAGER

MILLENNIUM FALCON

OCCUPATION: Former freighter turned revved-up smuggler

DATAPOINT: Her history is recounted in the novel *Star Wars: Millennium Falcon* by James Luceno.

SNAPSHOT: The *Millennium Falcon* began its life as a freighter, but it's come a long way since that humble start. Over the years, its owners—including Tobb Jadak, Lando Calrissian, and Han Solo—quietly upgraded her shields, weaponry, and engines to the point that she's likely now the fastest and most dangerous ship in her class. The *Falcon* has become a legend, due in no small part to pilot Han Solo's skills, both as a flyboy and teller of tall tales. It may look like a bucket of bolts, but she's got it where it counts.

VOYAGER

OCCUPATION: Fastest ship in Starfleet

DATAPOINT: *Star Trek: Voyager* was the first series in the franchise to use CGI, which meant the producers could dispense with cheesy-looking starship models.

SNAPSHOT: When launched on her maiden voyage, *Voyager* was the first ship in the Federation to be fitted with the new class-nine Warp drive, which allows her to sustain speeds just shy of Warp 10. On her first mission, an alien known as the Caretaker brought her all the way to the Delta Quadrant, 70,000 light-years away. Even as fast as *Voyager* is, making that return trip promises to take about 70 years to complete.

WHO'D WIN?

The *Millennium Falcon* is in trouble again. Han Solo has something on his ship that Captain Janeway of *Voyager* wants, and he would prefer to keep it. Figuring he can outrun Janeway's ship, Solo guns the *Falcon's* engines and starts making the calculations for the jump to hyperspace.

In-system, *Voyager* has the advantage. It can move at nearly 80 percent of light speed on its impulse engines, which it uses before making the jump to Warp speed. The *Falcon*, however, is far more maneuverable, and it can literally fly circles around the much larger *Voyager*, which boasts a crew complement of 160 people compared to the *Falcon's* two.

Once the *Falcon's* navigational computer kicks out the right numbers, though, the *Falcon* beats *Voyager* hands down. Any ship that can reach hyperspace speeds can travel over a million times the speed of light, making it possible to cross the entire galaxy in a matter of months. *Voyager*, on the other hand, can only reach up to 6,000 times the speed of light, which is why it'll take it so long to get home, even at maximum Warp.

RESULT: The *Millennium Falcon* takes this one, in less than twelve parsecs.

THE PILOTS

Surviving a starfight often comes down not to the capabilities of the ship but to the person flying it. This is especially true when you're talking about smaller craft like X-wings and TIE fighters, but it also applies with larger ships too. The fastest ship in the galaxy doesn't do you any good at all if you don't know how to fly it.

Fortunately, there's no dearth of excellent flyers in either Star Wars or Star Trek, so let's see what happens when we pit a couple of them against each other.

WEDGE ANTILLES VS. TOM PARIS

WEDGE ANTILLES

OCCUPATION: Starfighter pilot for the Rebel Alliance

DATAPOINT: Antilles was featured as a hero in the *Star Wars: X-Wing: Rogue Squadron* novels and comics by Michael A. Stackpole.

SNAPSHOT: Wedge Antilles, native of Corellia, is a crack pilot and a lucky man. Of all the members of Red Squadron that took part in the Battle of Yavin in which Luke Skywalker destroyed the Death Star, only Luke and he survived. Attribute that to Wedge's crackerjack piloting, which also helped him rack up six kills during the battle. From there he went on to found the Rogue Squadron. Wedge is widely recognized as one of the best pilots in the Rebel Alliance, and he works hard to maintain that reputation—and to survive what it takes to do that.

TOM PARIS

OCCUPATION: Flight controller of *Voyager*

DATAPOINT: Robert Duncan McNeill, who played Paris, also appeared on *Star Trek: The Next Generation* as a member of Starfleet Academy intent on covering something up.

SNAPSHOT: Thomas Eugene Paris is a brash and sometimes arrogant man whose piloting error once killed three Starfleet crewmen and got him drummed out of Starfleet. He later spent time in prison for joining the Maquis, but wound up helping *Voyager* go after the Maquis in return for his freedom. Trapped in the Delta Quadrant with *Voyager*, he became the ship's flight controller and recently became the first person to break the Warp 10 barrier.

WHO'D WIN?

Tom Paris beams down to Yavin to infiltrate the Rebel base and see what he can learn about the situation in this part of the galaxy. When he hears the Rebels' story, he sympathizes with their underdog status and volunteers to join as a pilot. He's assigned to Red Squadron, which lost nearly all its pilots in the battle that destroyed the Death Star. Before he can make it official, though, he needs to fly against Wedge and show off his stuff.

Paris takes off in a borrowed X-wing and faces off against Wedge in an identical craft. The game is Follow the Leader, and Wedge is in the front position. Wedge leads Paris through a series of ever more demanding stunts and maneuvers, and Paris manages to keep up through every bit of it. Then Paris decides he doesn't want to play the follower any more. He wants to be the leader.

Paris guns the engine and tries to leap in front of Wedge. To do this, he coaxes both his fighter and Wedge into a power dive that should put him in the lead. Unfortunately, the fighters run out of sky before he manages to take the lead. Wedge pulls up just in time, but Tom's too determined to win and has to eject from the fighter an instant before it crashes into the ground.

RESULT: Tom won the battle but lost the war. Wedge takes this one.

THE FIGHTERS

While battles between massive starships count for a great deal in both sagas, some of the most exciting battles involve smaller ships: fighters, shuttlecraft, and the like. In dogfights, the skill and determination of a single pilot means far more in the course of the battle than they would to the helmsman of a larger ship, which gives its controller a far greater margin of error. Pilots of small and nimble craft have no one but themselves to rely on—it's far more personal.

X-WING VS. JEM'HADAR FIGHTER

X-WING

OCCUPATION: Starfighter favored by the Rebel Alliance

DATAPOINT: The X-Wing took a starring role in the first Star Wars flight simulation game *Star Wars: X-Wing* in 1993.

SNAPSHOT: The Incom T-65 X-wing is the most famous starfighter in the Star Wars universe. Red Squadron flew all X-wings on its mission to destroy the Death Star. Luke Skywalker flew his to Dagobah—and crashed it into a swamp. Yoda showed him the power of the Force by levitating it out of the muck.

The X-wing is fast, durable, maneuverable, and comes with plenty of shielding and weaponry. It's the iconic starfighter of its age, and it earned that reputation well.

JEM'HADAR FIGHTER

OCCUPATION: Dominion light attack ship

DATAPOINT: Jem'Hadar ships don't have a central viewscreen on the bridge. Only the ship's commanders permitted to view what's going on outside the ship.

SNAPSHOT: The Federation rarely bothers with starfighters, preferring instead to focus on larger ships like the *Enterprise, Voyager,* or *Defiant.* Smaller ships have a hard time harming such behemoths because of their superior shielding and sheer mass. However, smaller ships do have other purposes, and trying to take out a starfighter with a capital ship can be like trying to kill a horde of mosquitoes with a sledgehammer. During the Dominion War, the Federation was harried by the Jem'Hadar fighters. Fast and maneuverable, they were sent after Federation starships in swarms.

WHO'D WIN?

While zipping through the galaxy in his X-wing, Luke Skywalker dumps out of hyperspace near a wormhole that didn't show up on his navicomputer's star charts. Ensign Nog, out on patrol around Deep Space Nine in a Federation runabout, is being chased down by a better armed Jem'Hadar fighter. Luke knows an unfair fight when he sees one, but before he can act, the Jem'Hadar fighter lines up his X-wing in its sights and opens fire with its directed energy array.

Luke spins his X-wing into an evasive maneuver, dodging the attack and zooming past the Jem'Hadar fighter as he pulls a stunt that leaves Nog agape at the X-wing's nimble nature.

Nog tries to bring his runabout around to get a closer look at the X-wing, but before he can manage it, he discovers that the Jem'Hadar fighter is back on his tail.

Ignoring his targeting computer, Luke lines up his shot and pulls the trigger of his quadruple laser cannons. The lasers light up the Jem'Hadar fighter, and Nog is in the clear.

RESULT: The disparate skill of the pilots aside, the X-wing outclasses the Jem'Hadar.

LOADED FOR WAR

Some ships are meant to protect their occupants. Others are built for speed. A few, though, come armed to the teeth, determined to do as much destruction in a dogfight as they can in as short a time as possible. They sit somewhere between the massive capital ships and the nimble fighters, rugged scrappers that can take it as well as they can dish it out.

SLAVE I VS. DELTA FLYER

SLAVE I

OCCUPATION: Personal spacecraft for the most dangerous bounty hunter in the galaxy

DATAPOINT: Rumors that its shape was inspired by a street lamp are entirely unfounded.

SNAPSHOT: You won't find a ship like *Slave I* on the assembly line of any starship manufacturer. It's what a car collector would consider a classic: it may have its adherents, but it's long out of date. Originally the ship belonged to Jango Fett, who refurbished it stem to stern with the latest in shielding, weaponry, and stealth systems, and his son Boba Fett carries on that tradition, making it the toughest and sneakiest ship in known space. The most striking thing about *Slave I* is that the pilot has to stand upright while flying it, right between the massive cannon systems mounted on the ship's shoulders.

DELTA FLYER

OCCUPATION: Battle-ready shuttlecraft flown out of *Voyager*

DATAPOINT: First seen in the *Star Trek: Voyager* episode "Extreme Risk."

SNAPSHOT: After *Voyager* was trapped in the Delta Quadrant, Tom Paris realized that the shuttlecraft they had on board the ship weren't going to cut it. They needed something tougher for the times they needed to send a team out in a smaller vessel. To that end, the crew designed and built the *Delta Flyer*, a tricked-out shuttle that could handle itself in a rough crowd. After the Borg destroyed the first *Delta Flyer*, *Voyager's* crew built another one to replace it right away.

WHO'D WIN?

Boba Fett sets out to collect a price that the wealthy patron of an irate Dralian named Gar put on Neelix's head. Not being foolish enough to take on *Voyager* directly, Fett waits for Neelix to leave the ship in the *Delta Flyer* on one of his regular forays to restock *Voyager's* pantry. The moment the *Delta Flyer* is distant enough that *Voyager* can no longer protect it, Fett zooms in with *Slave I* and attacks.

The *Delta Flyer's* duranium hull protects Neelix from the first round of blasts from *Slave I's* twin laser cannons, but just barely. He has time to return fire with the ship's pulse phased weapons, but *Slave I's* shields absorb them long enough for Fett to let loose a pair of proton torpedoes. Neelix tries to go to Warp to avoid the torpedoes, but they catch up to the *Delta Flyer* before he can manage it, and the engines of the muscled-up shuttlecraft go up in a bright ball of light.

Neelix better hope Captain Janeway can pay his ransom.

RESULT: Boba Fett always gets his man.

CAPITAL SHIPS

Dogfighting starships make for fast-paced action, but if you want a truly epic conflict, you have to haul out the big guns. In this case, that means some of the largest ships ever seen—anything shy of a space station. Individually, any one of these ships could flatten an entire city. Working together, they could destroy a planet.

It's when they face off against each other that the big booms really start to fly.

EXECUTOR VS. *ENTERPRISE-E*

EXECUTOR

OCCUPATION: Destroying thousands of Rebel scum at a time

DATAPOINT: This giant ship first commands the spaceways in *Star Wars: The Empire Strikes Back.*

SNAPSHOT: The *Executor* is Darth Vader's command ship, an Imperial Star Dreadnought that dwarfs most ships in the Imperial fleet or any other. (The Death Star and Death Star II are technically space stations.) Its arrowhead-shaped hull stretches nearly 12 miles long from stem to stern, and it features over 5,000 weapon emplacements in addition to the dozens of smaller craft stationed on the ship. When Vader is not aboard the ship, command of it falls to Admiral Piett. Like most of Vader's officers, he lives in mortal fear of disappointing the Sith Lord.

ENTERPRISE-E

OCCUPATION: To boldly go where no one has gone before

DATAPOINT: The *Enterprise-E* makes its maiden voyage in the movie *Star Trek: Nemesis.*

SNAPSHOT: The *Enterprise (NCC-1701-E)* is the sixth ship in the service of the Federation to bear that name and number—seventh if you count the *NX-01.* Like each of the *Enterprise*s before it, it is

Starfleet's flagship, the pride of the entire fleet. It stretches almost half a mile long, has sixteen phaser arrays and ten torpedo tubes, and has a total of twenty-nine decks. Where she leads, Starfleet follows.

WHO'D WIN?

"Dear God," Captain Picard says as the _Executor_, which has just popped out of hyperspace over Earth, appears on the _Enterprise's_ viewscreen. "What is it?"

"It is the largest ship ever recorded, sir," says Data. "Although not as thick, it is more than six times as long as a Borg cube and at least as well armed."

"Hailing frequencies."

Darth Vader appears on the viewscreen.

"I am Captain Jean-Luc Picard of the United Federation of Planets. What is the nature of your visit?"

"I am here to welcome you, Captain."

Picard allows himself an uncertain smile. "Should we not be welcoming you? You are on the doorstep of our home planet."

"Yes. That is why we are here: to welcome your Federation _to the Empire!_"

"They are arming weapons, sir."

"Shields up! Mr. Data, get us out of here!"

"I'm trying sir, but they seem to have caught us in some sort of tractor beam."

"Full reverse!"

"It's no good," says Commander Riker. "We're not gaining an inch."

"Fine," says Picard as a swarm of TIE fighters pours out of the great dreadnought. "If they want the _Enterprise_ so much, let's give it to them. Full impulse ahead, Mr. Data. Aim for their bridge."

RESULT: The _Executor_ earns its name today.

OUR RUNNING TALLY

Starships

	SAGA THIS CHAPTER	RUNNING TALLY
Star Wars	5	28
Star Trek	0	24
Ties	0	3

Here's where Star Wars just spanks Star Trek and sends it to bed without a kiss from its momma. Star Trek's closer adherence to science probably hurts it here. Its starships may be more realistic, but that just means they're not as cool, either.

PART III

TIME AND SPACE

What good is a starship if you have no place to go? Here's a chance to test your stellar cartography skills.

1. **The Rebel base in danger of destruction at the end of _Star Wars: A New Hope_ is based on a moon known as:**
   A. Endor
   B. Yavin 4
   C. Hoth
   D. Coruscant

2. **The United Federation of Planets is based on Earth, in the city of:**
   A. San Francisco
   B. New York
   C. Rome
   D. Beijing

3. **The capital planet of both the Galactic Republic and the Galactic Empire is:**
   A. Vulcan
   B. Coruscant
   C. Tatooine
   D. Alderaan

4. **The pleasure planet popular for R&R among _Next Generation_ Starfleet officers is called:**
   A. Xindi
   B. Cardassia
   C. Orion
   D. Risa

5. **When threatened with the destruction of Alderaan by the Death Star, Princess Leia Organa informs Grand Moff Tarkin that the Rebel base is on:**
   A. Pluto
   B. Endor
   C. Dantooine
   D. Coruscant

6. **In _Star Trek (2009)_, the Romulan Nero destroys the planet:**
   A. Vulcan
   B. Earth
   C. Romulus
   D. Hoth

Answers: 1. B, 2. A, 3. B, 4. D, 5. C, 6. A

CHAPTER 12

PLANETS
There's Always Just One More to Explore

While much of the action in both Star Wars and Star Trek takes place on ships, eventually someone has to go down to a planet to check it out or grab supplies. Each universe has a wide variety of amazing planets, from lifeless hunks of rock to jungle planets. But which planets would we most like to visit?

THE CAPITAL PLANETS

Some planets are just more important than others. Eventually even Superman has to leave Smallville and head for Metropolis because that's where his destiny lies: in the big city, where everything's happening. The same goes for farm boys everywhere, whether you're from Iowa or Tatooine.

CORUSCANT VS. EARTH

CORUSCANT

OCCUPATION: Seat of government for both the Republic and the Empire

DATAPOINT: Coruscant was first mentioned in the novel *Star Wars: Heir to the Empire* by Timothy Zahn.

SNAPSHOT: The most heavily populated planet in the galaxy pulses with sentient life at every instant of the day. Coruscant has been the hotbed of galactic civilization for thousands of years, and there's no sign that this will ever change. The Jedi Temple is located here, as is the Galactic Senate. Flying cars speed about everywhere in layers of congested traffic, and the buildings reach miles into the sky. People from every other habitable planet and every walk of life stroll the streets of Coruscant and jet from one place to another. It truly is the jewel in the Republic's crown.

EARTH

OCCUPATION: Birthplace of humanity and center of the United Federation of Planets

DATAPOINT: The first mention of the Federation, a body that includes 150 members, was in the 1967 episode of *Star Trek: The Original Series*, "A Taste of Armageddon."

SNAPSHOT: Earth is a relative paradise in the twenty-fourth century. With a nearly unlimited supply of nonpolluting, power-driving replicators, this is a world without want that cares not only about its people but their environment. Despite serving as the home for Starfleet and the Federation, Earth still features wide swathes of pristine wilderness seemingly unharmed by any of the multitude of fears we have for the environment today.

WHO'D WIN?

"Will," Deanna Troi says, "where would you like to go for our honeymoon? Coruscant or Earth?"

"I thought we were going to Risa."

"Weren't you banned from there the last time you visited?"

"I'm sure they've forgotten about that by now. If a man helps save the galaxy, they tend to overlook such details."

"Seriously, Earth or Coruscant?"

"Well, we've never been to Coruscant before. It sounds exciting."

"Yes," Troi says, "perhaps too much. It sounds like a wonderful place if you're among the wealthy and powerful, but what about all the people who have to live in the lower levels? Can they even see the sun?"

"I don't think we'll wind up staying in the lower levels."

"Wouldn't you rather spend a week in Hawaii than in the area around the Galactic Senate or the Jedi Temple?"

"Hm." Riker rubs his clean-shaven face. "Politics and religion, or a warm, pristine beach. I think you've sold me on this one, but you already knew that, didn't you?"

"Yes." Troi smiles. "Yes, I did."

RESULT: Earth beats Coruscant hollow. Not that Coruscant's hollow. As far as we know.

ICE PLANETS

Ice planets are so cold that they present a hazard to anyone who sets foot on them. Temperatures can drop so low as to guarantee frostbite, hypothermia, and death to those who stay out unprotected for too long. Their shifting winds and regular blizzard conditions make it hard for anyone to see what's happening on the surface—or to detect the creatures sneaking up on you to steal your warmth and with it your life.

HOTH VS. DELTA VEGA

HOTH

OCCUPATION: Frozen planet on which sits a large Rebel base

DATAPOINT: Hoth, backdrop of the opening sequence of *Star Wars: The Empire Strikes Back,* is the sixth planet of the Hoth system, located in the Outer Rim Territories.

SNAPSHOT: Hoth houses the Rebels' main base after they have to light out of Yavin 4 at the end of *Star Wars: A New Hope.* The reason it seems to have been chosen as the place least likely for the Empire to look for the Rebels is because it's so damned cold there, the only rational answer to "Let's go to Hoth" is "You must be joking." Hoth has its own kind of beauty, but it also has its own kind of killing and eating machine: the wampa.

DELTA VEGA

OCCUPATION: Icy planet on which you'd think it would be safe to abandon Starfleet officers

DATAPOINT: Kirk and the original Spock are stranded here in *Star Trek (2009)*.

SNAPSHOT: Delta Vega is a barely habitable planet in the Vulcan system that orbits slightly farther out from its central star than the planet Vulcan does. In fact, the orbits are close enough that it's possible—at least part of the time—to see Vulcan riding high in the Delta Vega sky during daytime hours. Starfleet has a small outpost here, but the place is otherwise mostly abandoned, the exception being marooned Starfleet officers who somehow seem to turn up within easy walking distance of the outpost.

WHO'D WIN?

"I can't believe you were stuck on this ice ball for the past six months, Scotty," says Kirk. "How'd you manage to survive?"

"You don't really think that Starfleet, in all its infinite wisdom and glory, would just abandon me here without any food or drink now, do you?"

"Well," Kirk says, pondering the thought, "that is how both I and Ambassador Spock wound up here. You think that's a coincidence?"

"More like the people who abandoned you here wanted you to be able to watch Vulcan be destroyed, but be sure you'd find your way to this station for the sake of your health."

"Maybe I should have just stayed in my escape pod," Kirk grumbles

"What, and miss out on all the fun of getting chased around the ice by the not-so-wee beasties that live on and under it?" Scotty replies. "Nah. Besides, you think that big crab-thing couldn't have just swallowed you like the tiny morsel you'd be to it?"

"Great. So where would you rather be?"

"Well, now that you mention it, I hear Hoth is a slightly better ice planet to be stuck on, as ice planets go. At least the monsters there aren't so damned big."

RESULT: If you're looking for the scariest of the iciest planets around, Delta Vega wins the prize.

THE WORST FATE

In many a science fiction saga, the fate of an entire planet may be at stake. In *Star Wars: A New Hope*, the Death Star destroys one home-world and threatens others. Red matter does the same in *Star Trek (2009)*. But which planet's destruction made the most impact and the most spectacular *kaboom?*

ALDERAAN VS. VULCAN

ALDERAAN

OCCUPATION: Homeworld of Leia Organa and convenient target

DATAPOINT: Although much is made in *Star Wars: A New Hope* about the Death Star's ability to destroy entire planets, Alder-aan is the only one that gets blown up—which sucks for the Alderaanians.

SNAPSHOT: Alderaan is a peaceful world, having disarmed itself after the ravages the Clone Wars wreaked upon it. Officially, it is part of the Empire, and Princess Leia Organa is the planet's repre-sentative in the Senate that the Emperor dissolves shortly before the destruction of the planet. Grand Moff Tarkin uses the Death Star to blow up Alderaan and make a statement about the Empire's new superweapon and what will happen to any who dare defy the Emperor.

VULCAN

OCCUPATION: Homeworld to the most logical sentient species in the galaxy

DATAPOINT: When Nero manages to inject red matter into Vulcan, the planet implodes in the movie *Star Trek (2009)*.

SNAPSHOT: Vulcan is the homeworld of the pointy-eared, green-blooded logic-mongers named after their planet. It's a harsh, arid place filled with deserts and volcanoes, but it has its own stark beauty about it. The Vulcans strive to maintain tight control over their emotions and employ cold-hearted logic to all problems. In the end, this did nothing to save their planet, but then, what could?

WHO'D WIN?

At the moment of its destruction, Alderaan held about two billion people. Its destruction came as a complete surprise to everyone on the planet. One moment the people of Alderaan are going about their day, minding their own business, and a moment later there's a space station the size of a moon sitting in their sky. Not too long after that, there's a big flash of light from the Death Star's laser dish, and the entire planet goes *boom*.

Vulcan, on the other hand, was one of the great centers of learning and knowledge in the galaxy and served as home to six billion people at the time of its destruction. When Nero showed up to destroy it, he first ambushed a large force of starships sent by Starfleet to save the day. Then he set up a massive drill that bored a hole into the center of the planet. Only when that was complete did he fire the red matter into the hole. As the black hole Nero created at Vulcan's core began to form, it swallowed the planet over the course of many horrifying minutes rather than taking it out in a flash.

RESULT: Vulcan's destruction made for a far more dramatic moment. Sadly, it wins.

DIPLOMATS

Diplomats play the role of grease in the gears of galactic politics. They negotiate treaties between worlds, and their machinations often provide the impetus for adventures, raising the stakes from personal to planetary to galactic.

NUTE GUNRAY VS. SAREK

NUTE GUNRAY

OCCUPATION: Viceroy of the Trade Federation and treacherous slime

DATAPOINT: Introduced in the movie *Star Wars: The Phantom Menace*, he rose to power after the Stark Hyperspace War as described in the *Star Wars: Republic* series.

SNAPSHOT: As the Viceroy of the Trade Federation, Nute Gunray set up the blockade and invasion of Naboo in conjunction with help from Darth Sidious. Though the Jedi defeated him and brought him to justice, Gunray managed to avoid any serious repercussions for his actions and resumed his work with the Trade Federation with little interruption. He and Sidious are now hoping to set up the Confederacy of Independent Systems to further his ambitions, but more than anything else he wants Padmé Amidala dead.

SAREK

OCCUPATION: Vulcan ambassador for the Federation, father to Spock

DATAPOINT: We meet him for the first time in the *Star Trek: The Original Series* episode "Journey to Babel."

SNAPSHOT: In his more than 120 years in this galaxy, few people have done as much as Sarek to further the cause of peace through diplomatic means. His logic is flawless, and his arguments are convincing without stirring emotions. He spent many years estranged from his half-human son Spock after the youth joined Starfleet, but the two eventually reconciled. In the aftermath of Spock's death and return to life, they became closer than ever.

WHO'D WIN?

Nute Gunray enters the meeting room on Risa where Ambassador Sarek is waiting for him and says, "Thank you for agreeing to meet with me."

"Of course," Sarek replies. "My research tells me that your Trade Federation appears to be a large power in your region. It only makes sense for us to talk openly. You are interested in having the Federation join your Trade Federation?"

"That is our hope."

"I don't believe I can make that happen," Sarek states.

"What? Why not?"

"You gain a great deal of your support from a man who calls himself Darth Sidious."

"How do you know that?"

"That's not the issue," Sarek coldly replies.

Gunray frowns deeper. "So what is the issue then? Why did you haul me all the way out here? Just to throw this in my face?"

Sarek waits for Gunray to calm down. Then he speaks. "I wish to share some information with you that might prevent you from making a horrible mistake."

Gunray stifles his angry response and nods for Sarek to go on.

"Are you aware that Darth Sidious is, in fact, your Senator Palpatine? That he is using you and your Trade Federation to bolster support for himself in the Galactic Senate? And that when he has garnered that support he will likely cut you loose?"

"Whaaattt?" Gunray puts his fists on the table between them. "This is an outrage and a pack of lies. How could you possibly know any of that?"

"It's easy enough to piece together from even the barest of facts." Sarek shrugs. "Logic, Viceroy Gunray. Logic."

RESULT: Sarek schools Gunray—and perhaps saves his life at the same time.

PLANETARY GOVERNORS

Both Star Wars and Star Trek feature interplanetary governments that control at least a portion of the galaxy. It's impossible for any ruling body to manage direct control over so many billions of people. That job falls to the planetary governors instead, the men and women either appointed or elected to govern their people and represent them in the interstellar government. These people have a great deal of power, but it's how they use that power that matters most.

BAIL ORGANA VS. GUL DUKAT

BAIL ORGANA

OCCUPATION: Head of the Royal Family of Alderaan and eminent politician

DATAPOINT: Bail Organa was first mentioned as Prestor Organa in the Star Wars radio drama, circa 1981.

SNAPSHOT: Bail Organa may have been born to his position, but he did his best every day to fill it as if he'd been elected to it. He worked long and hard to try to preserve the Republic, and now that the Empire has finally been established, he hopes to work within its parameters to effect change and help as many people as he can. He recently adopted a baby girl, Leia, whom he knows is secretly the daughter of his old friend Padmé Amidala of Naboo and her husband, Anakin Skywalker.

GUL DUKAT

OCCUPATION: Politician and occasional ruler of Cardassia

DATAPOINT: Before playing Gul Dukat on *Star Trek: Deep Space Nine*, actor Marc Alaimo appeared as the first Cardassian seen onscreen—Gul Macet—on *Star Trek: The Next Generation*.

SNAPSHOT: The former Cardassian prefect of Bajor, Dukat has plenty of experience ruling over a planet with an iron fist. He also ran Terok Nor, later known as Deep Space Nine, so he knows the region and his enemies and allies well. Sensing a chance to return to power, Dukat secretly negotiated for Cardassia to join the Dominion, installing himself as the leader of his home planet. He is, at the moment, a popular leader who promises to restore Cardassia to its former glory.

WHO'D WIN?

Bail Organa has agreed to meet in secret with Gul Dukat on Coruscant. He hopes that Dukat might be a powerful ally against the Empire, and he hopes to learn more about Cardassia and the Dominion, which Dukat claims to represent. They rendezvous in Dex's Diner.

"I'm pleased you agreed to meet me during my stay on Coruscant," says Dukat.

"It's the least I could do," says Organa. "Tell me more about this Dominion of yours. What do they hope to achieve?"

"Everlasting peace, of course." Dukat smiles. "We are both men of the galaxy. We know how hard that is to achieve. That's why we are actively pursuing alliances with others to further our goals."

Organa strokes his beard. "What if I told you that I could put you in touch with a group of senators who would be only too happy to find such support for their planets—outside of the Empire?"

Dukat's grin grows. "I'd say you show yourself to be a traitor to the allies we've already established in this part of the galaxy."

Surprised, Organa follows Dukat's gaze outside the diner's windows to see that stormtroopers have surrounded the place. Organa snarls at Dukat, but the Cardassian only tut-tuts at him. "Now, Senator, I'm sure we can work out a deal. After all, if you're executed, who's going to look after your precious little girl?"

RESULT: Dukat's treachery triumphs—for now.

OUR RUNNING TALLY

Planets

	SAGA THIS CHAPTER	RUNNING TALLY
Star Wars	0	28
Star Trek	5	29
Ties	0	3

Star Trek leaps out of its bedroom, grabs Star Wars, gives it a matter-antimatter wedgie, and tosses it out into the front yard. The planets of Star Trek consistently outranked those in Star Wars, but then again, it's right there in the name. Star Trek is a travel show, right?

From Skylab to Mir to the International Space Station, orbiting outposts have long been a part of both science fiction and science fact, and Star Wars and Star Trek both have their share of space stations. Care to test your memory?

1. **The Imperial officer whom Darth Vader choked because he found his lack of faith disturbing was:**
   A. Admiral Motti
   B. Grand Moff Tarkin
   C. Admiral Ackbar
   D. Owen Lars

2. **In *Star Trek II: The Wrath of Khan*, the Genesis Device was developed on:**
   A. Ceti Alpha V
   B. Space Station Regula 1
   C. Deep Space Nine
   D. Yavin 4

3. **When the heroes on the *Millennium Falcon* first see the Death Star, they mistake it for a:**
   A. Moon
   B. Planet
   C. Star
   D. Ewok

4. **Soon after the Federation took over Deep Space Nine, the space station was moved close to a wormhole near the planet:**
   A. Earth
   B. Cardassia
   C. Romulus
   D. Bajor

5. **The diameter of the Death Star II was how much larger than that of the original Death Star?**
   A. Twice
   B. Three times
   C. Four times
   D. More than five times

6. **The original name of Deep Space Nine when the Cardassians created it was:**
   A. Gateway to the Prophets
   B. Deep Space Nine
   C. Dukat Station
   D. Terok Nor

Answers: 1. A, 2. B, 3. A, 4. D, 5. D, 6. D

CHAPTER 13

SPACE STATIONS
Home Away From Home

In space, sometimes they don't have a planet right where you need it. Or maybe it's just not so wise to set foot directly on the ground—nearby there are monsters out there, and acidic atmospheres, and all sorts of nasty stuff. Hanging out forever in a ship in the middle of nowhere often isn't a good option though, so what should you do?

Build yourself a space station, of course.

THE LEADERS

A space station is only as good as the person who leads it. Unlike a city or a business, a space station can't just coast along as a place that people pass through. It has to have a purpose, or it just winds up abandoned, a floating monument to someone else's failed ambitions spiraling through space. A strong leader can give such a station a purpose—or repurpose it from its original intent to become something new.

GRAND MOFF TARKIN VS. BENJAMIN SISKO

GRAND MOFF TARKIN

OCCUPATION: Imperial governor of the Outland Regions, commander of the Death Star

DATAPOINT: He was the originator of the Tarkin Doctrine, which called for ruling the universe through fear and intimidation, backed up by superweapons such as the Death Star.

SNAPSHOT: Grand Moff Tarkin is a ruthless bastard whose loyalty to the Emperor is as unquestioned as his complete lack of empathy for any who would try to resist his rule. He believes that the best way to cow rebels is to kill them in such a spectacular way as to cause anyone thinking of following in their footsteps to question their personal judgment. He takes advantage of his shock-and-awe powers whenever he can, and so far it has served him well, both terrifying his opposition and improving his standing in the Emperor's eyes.

BENJAMIN SISKO

OCCUPATION: Starfleet commander

DATAPOINT: The series *Star Trek: Deep Space Nine* began with the 1993 pilot episode "Emissary," which suggested that Sisko might be a major religious figure to Bajorans.

SNAPSHOT: Benjamin Sisko has often considered leaving Starfleet behind, but as hard as the life of an officer has sometimes been on both himself and his son, Jake, he knows he can do the most good for the most people on Deep Space Nine, so he stays. He has struggled with the loss of his wife, Jennifer, to the Borg, but his work has helped ease the pain. He takes his job seriously, though himself less so. Sisko is a man of honor who cares about getting good results, but he's not willing to dispose of his personal principles to achieve them.

WHO'D WIN?

Captain Sisko and Grand Moff Tarkin share a drink at the bar after a long day of seminars at the Space Station Commanders Conference.

"No, no, no, old man," Sisko says. "You can't treat them like that. You've got to get them on your side."

"What do I care what my officers think of me?" says Tarkin. "I issue my orders, and they obey. Or I make a very painful example of them."

"But if you rule through terror, if you make them keep their heads down, they might never be able to show you what you're missing. You might not even be able to see it yourself."

"I watch carefully. I see everything."

Sisko shakes his head. "That's not possible. You can't be everywhere at once. That's why you're so worried about those stolen plans. Someone out there might find something you missed because you were too busy doing other things to spot it. You've got to learn to delegate. Get your people to trust you, to work *for* you, not against you."

"Bah," Tarkin says. "I should introduce you to Lord Vader and let the two of you debate your feelings together."

"Keep thinking that way," Sisko says with a sly grin, "and someday you might find that 'ultimate power in the galaxy' of yours blown out from underneath you."

RESULT: Sisko takes this one. He didn't later have his space station destroyed, killing everyone on board, after all.

SECURITY

One of the most important elements of any space station is its security. A hunk of pressurized environment floating in open space is a disaster waiting to happen. It doesn't take much for everything to go horribly, spiral-into-the-nearest-sun wrong. It's up to the space station's security team to prevent that from happening, or at least to make it as hard as possible.

ZAM WESELL VS. ODO

ZAM WESELL

OCCUPATION: Shapeshifting assassin

DATAPOINT: Zam was featured in her own Dark Horse Comics graphic novel, *Star Wars: Zam Wesell* by Ron Marz and Ted Naifeh.

SNAPSHOT: Zam Wesell doesn't have anything to do with protecting a space station or any other sort of property. More like the opposite of that. She's a stone-cold killer who, as part of her Clawdite heritage, happens to be able to morph her appearance so she can look like anyone else. As you can imagine, this is one hell of an asset for a contract killer.

ODO

OCCUPATION: Chief of security for Deep Space Nine

DATAPOINT: Odo was falsely accused of murder in the *Star Trek: Deep Space Nine* episode "A Man Alone."

SNAPSHOT: Odo is a changeling sent out into the galaxy by the Founders as an infant to explore and report back—but he worked as security chief on Deep Space Nine for a while before he knew that. For years all he knew was that he didn't know where he came from or why he can do the things he can do. He's all alone in the universe, but despite that he's found a vocation in protecting others from harm.

WHO'D WIN?

Zam Wesell arrives on Deep Space Nine, posing as a beautiful woman and hunting for her latest prey. She decides to check with the chief of security to see if he might know Padmé Amidala's whereabouts. If someone as important as her is moved through the station, news would be sure to get out. Odo is too busy to deal with someone merely passing through the space station, but Wesell's question intrigues him and prods his investigative mind into action. After speaking with her for a minute, he realizes that she's not who—or *what*—she claims to be.

"You're a changeling," he says in awe. "Your eyes. I just saw them change shades—and shapes."

"That's impossible."

"Not at all," he says. "Just terribly uncommon." He grabs her by the shoulders. "Who are you? Where are you from? Tell me!"

Disturbed that Odo might destroy her cover and with it her ability to function anywhere in the space station, she decides to drop the facade. "It's true," she says as she reverts to her reptilian-humanoid form. "I'm not from around here. But then neither are you."

"Tell me more," he said. "Tell me about myself. Please."

"All right," Wesell said. "I know one thing about you that you don't know yet."

"What's that?"

Wesell jams a blaster against Odo's head. "You're dead."

RESULT: Wesell finds Odo's weak spot and exploits it to deadly effect.

MEDICAL FACILITIES

A space station is a long way away from the nearest hospital, but it serves as a waystation for every starship that passes through the region. Because of that, the station needs to have its own medical care facilities on board. Otherwise, those who have to wait to get to a planet's surface may simply die.

IT-O INTERROGATOR DROID VS. DR. JULIAN BASHIR

IT-O INTERROGATOR DROID

OCCUPATION: Interrogation droid

DATAPOINT: The IT-O model used in filming *A New Hope* in 1977 had "British made" written on its hypodermic needle.

SNAPSHOT: The IT-O Interrogator was designed for a single purpose, and it's frighteningly good at its job. It uses scientifically administered pain and drugs to force information out of its subjects. Using medical technology, it carefully scans its victims to determine the best and most efficient way to induce pain. It also uses its medical knowledge to keep the target alive under even the harshest conditions for as long as possible, often well past the victim's breaking point.

DR. JULIAN BASHIR

OCCUPATION: Starfleet medical officer assigned to Deep Space Nine

DATAPOINT: Alexander Siddig, who played Bashir, was personally involved with two *Star Trek* actors: Nana Vistor, to whom he was married from 1997 to 2001, and Kim Cattrall.

SNAPSHOT: Julian Bashir was a slow child—right up until his parents paid to have his DNA illegally resequenced, transforming him into a genius. As a doctor, he's always been on the hunt for new challenges and new arenas in which he can do the most good. He believes Deep Space Nine fits that bill. Bashir is sharp, witty, and ready to dig in and do the hard work when required.

WHO'D WIN?

The IT-O droid moves in and injects Dr. Bashir with a perfectly measured dose of sodium pentothal, and the Starfleet officer feels his resolve start to melt away. Due to his medical training, he knows exactly what the droid is capable of doing to him, but that doesn't make it any easier to resist its efforts to break him. Instead, it forces him to realize that he doesn't stand a chance of holding his tongue if the droid is prepared to shake it hard enough.

"I'll ask you one more time, Doctor," Gul Dukat says from where he stands behind the droid. "What have you done with the plans for the Death Star? My new friends in the Empire are desperate to find out."

"I don't know," Bashir says. "I've never seen them. I wish I had. I swear to you, it's the truth."

"How sad for you then, Doctor," Dukat says, "because that particular truth of yours is unacceptable, but for me to prove that, well, I'm afraid this is really going to hurt."

RESULT: The IT-O breaks Bashir soon enough. He's a good man, but it's not like he's trying to protect an entire rebellion.

MAINTENANCE

A space station is a large and wildly complicated machine, and it doesn't take much for it to begin falling apart. The person on the front line in the space station's war against chaos is its chief of operations. It's his or her job to keep the place running in tip-top condition and to be prepared for any eventuality. If the chief of operations fails—even at something that seems as remotely possible as having someone fire a torpedo down an unprotected shaft—the entire place could fall apart. Or blow up spectacularly.

DIANOGA VS. MILES O'BRIEN

DIANOGA

OCCUPATION: Trash monster

DATAPOINT: The monster originated on the planet Vodran and made only a single appearance, in *Star Wars: A New Hope*.

SNAPSHOT: A dianoga is a garbage-eating giant squid with a single eyestalk that it uses like a periscope to scout out prey moving above it. Such creatures commonly find their way into trash compactors, sewers, and other filthy holes where they can feed upon the wealth of garbage they find. Most of the time, people are happy to keep the disgusting creatures contained and let them feast on their wastes, as dianogas offer a natural way to deal with organic refuse. It's only when the creatures grow too big or aggressive that most people bother to hunt them down.

MILES O'BRIEN

OCCUPATION: Chief of operations on Deep Space Nine

DATAPOINT: O'Brien explored Deep Space Nine's abandoned sister station in the *Star Trek: Deep Space Nine* episode "Empok Nor."

SNAPSHOT: Miles O'Brien has been a Starfleet officer for over twenty years, and he spent the last several as the transporter chief on the *Enterprise* under Captain Picard. His recent transfer to Deep Space Nine has put him in regular contact with the people he likes the least: Cardassians. He's coming to terms with that, though, and has dedicated himself to getting the space station in top working order. Part of that is repairing the damage the Cardassians did as they left the place, and another part is hunting down all the booby traps he fears they left behind. Despite this, he is a good man, an honorable officer who does his best at his job.

WHO'D WIN?

When O'Brien first hears rumors of a monster living in the trash compactor in the lower levels of Deep Space Nine, he dismisses it as the kind of urban legend you can often hear on any space station. When a few pets in the same region go missing, O'Brien becomes suspicious that perhaps there's something to the rumors after all. Gathering Odo, he heads down to the trash compactor to investigate.

When O'Brien and Odo poke around in the muck, the dianoga attacks. The Cardassians had made sure to keep the monster happy and fed, but they've been gone for a while now. The creature's hunger has made it desperate.

Fortunately for O'Brien, the dianoga attacks Odo first, and the changeling simply slips free of the monster's tentacles. As soon as Odo is clear, O'Brien hustles him back out through the compactor's access door and seals it behind him. Then he pushes the button that vents the entire contents of the room into outer space.

"Problem solved," O'Brien says with a tight grin.

RESULT: O'Brien takes the dianoga out with the rest of the trash.

THE SPACE STATION

The most basic means of comparing space stations is to consider each of them in their entirety. It's not always a fair comparison because each space station has its own reason for existing. Regula 1 is all about research. Deep Space Nine is there to keep the peace. The Death Star and Death Star II exist only to intimidate and destroy. If they do their jobs, can any of them be considered a failure?

Let's find out.

THE DEATH STAR VS. DEEP SPACE NINE

THE DEATH STAR

OCCUPATION: Destroyer of worlds

DATAPOINT: The final stages of the Death Star's construction are detailed in the novel *Star Wars: Death Star* by Michael Reaves and Steve Perry.

SNAPSHOT: The Death Star is Grand Moff Tarkin's contribution to the Empire and the greatest display to date of its overwhelming power. What planetary governor in his right mind would dare risk every life on his planet to stand up to a space station that could murder everyone on that planet in an instant? After all, that kind of failure is going to make it damned hard to get re-elected.

DEEP SPACE NINE

OCCUPATION: Peacekeeping outpost of the Federation

DATAPOINT: The series *Star Trek: Deep Space Nine* was created by Rick Berman and Michael Piller.

SNAPSHOT: Though Deep Space Nine is firmly in the hands of the Federation, it is still a point of contention with both the Cardassians and the Dominion. Only through the efforts of Captain Sisko and his command team has it remained in the hands of the Federation for so long. It's these people who have made Deep Space Nine what it is and determined what it has come to represent, far more than the station itself.

WHO'D WIN?

"What in hell is that?" Captain Sisko asks as he gazes up at the Death Star, which dumped out of hyperspace nearby just moments ago. It dwarfs Deep Space Nine, stretching more than 110 times as wide

"I don't know, sir," says Miles O'Brien. "Could it be the Borg?"

"I don't think so," says Kira Nerys. "Not even the Borg have a ship that big."

"Chief O'Brien," says Sisko, "open up a channel to it."

"They're already hailing us, sir."

Sisko nods at O'Brien, and the image of Grand Moff Tarkin appears on Sisko's viewscreen. "Benjamin, my friend, I'm afraid that we find ourselves at cross-purposes today," says Tarkin. "I have information that the Rebels I'm hunting have established a base on your planet Bajor. Because of that, it has to go."

"Go?" Sisko says. "What do you mean?"

Before Sisko finishes speaking, the Death Star's laser dish already starts to warm up.

"Wait," Sisko says. "Can't we talk about this?"

"I'm afraid not," says Tarkin. "When it comes to these Rebels, the time for talk is over. Please give Bajor your good-byes."

The laser dish powers up, and an electric green beam fires from the Death Star and destroys the planet.

RESULT: This isn't even close. Sisko may be the better commander, but there's no way Deep Space Nine could ever hold up next to the Death Star.

OUR RUNNING TALLY

Space Stations

	SAGA THIS CHAPTER	RUNNING TALLY
Star Wars	3	31
Star Trek	2	31
Ties	0	3

Star Wars takes a small edge here, mostly because the Death Star dominates all other space stations. The results even the numbers up, and now it's anyone's contest again.

Here's the fourteenth set of questions designed to test your knowledge about Star Trek and Star Wars. If you get all these right, you may just be a master of time and space.

1. **The Jedi Master who trained Qui-Gon Jinn was:**
   A. Yoda
   B. Mace Windu
   C. Count Dooku
   D. Obi-Wan Kenobi

2. **The Earth scientist who invented the first Warp drive known to humans was:**
   A. Jonathan Archer
   B. Zefram Cochrane
   C. Montgomery Scott
   D. Harry Kim

3. **The number of years (in fictional time) between the end of *Star Wars: Revenge of the Sith* and *Star Wars: A New Hope* is:**
   A. Thirty
   B. Twelve
   C. Sixteen
   D. Nineteen

4. **In *Star Trek: The Original Series*, the men in the Mirror Universe have an odd affinity for:**
   A. Klingon flesh
   B. Beards
   C. Quoting Shakespeare
   D. The Blues

5. **What, besides a hyperdrive, does a ship need to be able to travel safely through hyperspace?**
   A. Seat belts
   B. Tachyon generators
   C. A Force-sensitive navigator
   D. Precise calculations

6. **In *Star Trek*, ships can communicate instantaneously over vast distances by use of signals sent and received in:**
   A. Hyperspace
   B. The Warp
   C. Subspace
   D. The Woof

Answers: 1. C, 2. B, 3. D, 4. B, 5. D, 6. C

CHAPTER 14

TIME AND SPACE
They Wait for No One

Because both Star Wars and Star Trek are science fiction, it's only natural that they be concerned with both time and space. While Star Wars doesn't feature any time travel, the fact that the Republic spans thousands of years gives it a sense of depth hard to find in other stories. Conversely, Star Trek regularly uses time travel, loops, and anomalies to build up intrigue across the centuries. Let's take a look at these popular science fiction elements a bit more closely.

WIDER UNIVERSES

There's a lot more to a universe than you could possibly pack into a film or TV series. That becomes even more true when you start considering all the optional possibilities for universes that diverge a bit from the stated canon for each saga. Whole encyclopedias have been written on these subjects.

THE EXPANDED UNIVERSE VS. THE MIRROR UNIVERSE

In Star Wars, there's a wealth of information and stories that have never been admitted as part of the official canon, which is reserved for film and television stories that George Lucas himself has a hand in. For Star Trek, we have a number of different alternate timelines/universes. Let's examine a couple of the most popular deviations.

THE EXPANDED UNIVERSE

OCCUPATION: Explaining old things, and showing us new things too

DATAPOINT: Most fans consider that the Star Wars Expanded Universe began with the publication, in 1978, of the novel *Star Wars: Splinter of the Mind's Eye* by Alan Dean Foster.

SNAPSHOT: The Expanded Universe is the catchall term used to describe the licensed Star Wars stories and products that remain faithful to Lucasfilm's current interpretation of the Star Wars universe. This includes most of the video games, comics, novels, and other narrative materials that extend from and sometimes even improve upon the original. While much of this stuff cannot be considered "official" in the sense that it matches up with George Lucas's ultimate vision, it's good enough for most of the fans out there to truly enjoy. It stretches in time from 25,000 years before the Battle of Yavin to more than 140 years later.

THE MIRROR UNIVERSE

OCCUPATION: Making the bad guys good and the good guys bad

DATAPOINT: This universe was first explored in the *Star Trek: The Original Series* episode "Mirror, Mirror."

SNAPSHOT: The Mirror Universe is one that diverged from the standard Star Trek universe at some unknown point in the past. Despite this, the twinned universes have moved in similar, parallel ways, with the exception that the good guys are now the bad guys and vice versa. During *Star Trek: The Original Series*, the fascist

Terran Empire is the great human power instead of the democratic United Federation of Planets. Later, Regent Worf of the Klingon-Cardassian Alliance rules over all.

WHO'D WIN?

The Mirror Universe *Enterprise* enters an ion-charged wormhole and emerges into the Expanded Universe. There it stumbles upon Han Solo flying the Sun Crusher, a weapon the size of a starfighter that has the ability to destroy an entire star system. Mirror-Spock's scanners recognize it for what it is, and he alerts the captain as to its unprecedented power. Under Mirror-Kirk's orders, the *Enterprise* launches a full-scale assault on the Sun Crusher, determined to capture it and take it back to the Mirror Universe, where Kirk can use it to become the uncontested ruler of the galaxy.

Solo, of course, is not interested in letting anyone get their hands on the Sun Crusher, least of all some wannabe despot from a different galaxy in a mirrored version of another universe. He does his best to evade the *Enterprise,* but as a weapon the Sun Crusher isn't well built for evasive action. When the *Enterprise* catches the Sun Crusher in its tractor beam, Solo gets an all-too-familiar sick feeling in his gut.

Rather than be captured, Solo launches one of the Sun Crusher's payload of monstrous energy resonance torpedoes, each one of which is capable of destabilizing and destroying a star by causing it to go supernova. It strikes the *Enterprise,* and the starship is obliterated in a blinding blast of light. When Solo's vision clears, only the Sun Crusher's indestructible hull still remains.

RESULT: The Expanded Universe can kill you in many ways over tens of thousands of years. It wins.

ECHOES OF THE PAST

Both Star Trek and Star Wars feature long and well-developed histories spanning hundreds, even tens of thousands, of years. It shouldn't surprise you then that bits from the past often rise up to surprise the heroes again and again. While death in both sagas is usually permanent, it's often not as simple as that.

JANGO FETT VS. SELA

JANGO FETT

OCCUPATION: Bounty hunter

DATAPOINT: He is the star of *Star Wars Adventures: Jango Fett Vs. The Razor Eaters,* a novel for young readers by Ryder Windham.

SNAPSHOT: Jango Fett is a legendary bounty hunter from the planet Mandalore. He's so good at what he does that he was chosen to be the genetic template for the entire clone army the Kaminoans created for the Republic. Most of these clones were genetically altered to be more loyal and compliant with orders—better soldiers than bounty hunters—but as part of his payment for his services, Jango received a single unaltered clone he raises as his son, Boba Fett.

SELA

OCCUPATION: Romulan commander

DATAPOINT: Sela's origins lie in the events of the *Star Trek: The Next Generation* episode "Yesterday's Enterprise." Her first appearance was in the episode "The Mind's Eye."

SNAPSHOT: Sela is the spitting image of her mother, Tasha Yar, a Starfleet officer whose alternate timeline double wound up in the past, where she was captured by Romulans and forced to become the consort of a Romulan general. Despite her half-human heritage, Sela grew up to rocket through the ranks of the Romulan military. She's dedicated herself to destroying the alliance between the Federation and the Klingon Empire, to the advantage of the Romulans.

WHO'D WIN?

Sela enters her quarters on her Romulan starship. Her plans to use the attachments the crew of the *Enterprise* has for her mother, their lost crewmember Tasha Yar, have borne the bitter fruit she'd been hoping to force them to eat. With a little bit of luck, the Federation and the Klingon Empire should be at war with each other within the week.

Her communications monitor lights up, indicating she has an incoming transmission. She answers it to see a mysterious man in a silver helmet with blue trim looking back at her.

"Commander Sela?" the man says.

"What do you want?" she asks.

"You've made some powerful enemies back on Romulus, Sela. They don't care for the way you've taken to disrupting the Klingons' relationship with the Federation."

Sela snarls into the viewscreen. "And what if I don't care what they have to say?"

"It makes no difference, really," says Jango Fett.

There's a *thump* against the hull that comprises one wall of Sela's quarters.

"Why's that?" she says as she stares at that wall.

"Because your superiors on Romulus pay well. Three . . . two . . ."

The wall explodes before Fett even reaches "one." The last thing that goes through Sela's head as she's sucked out into space by the explosive decompression of her cabin is how unfair it is that she would die this way—but she isn't dead.

Encased in some kind of transparent body-bag, Sela can only struggle in vain as she's pulled aboard a mysterious ship of unknown configuration marked *Slave I*.

"Save your strength," the strange man says. "We'll be back at Romulus in no time."

RESULT: Jango always gets his prey—unless that prey is Mace Windu.

THE FABRIC OF THE UNIVERSE

The Star Wars and Star Trek universes work differently from each other in fundamental ways, right down to the nature of space and the fabric of their universes. This determines how ships travel faster than light, how the people of each universe communicate with each other instantly, and even if and how they can travel through time.

HYPERSPACE VS. SUBSPACE

HYPERSPACE

OCCUPATION: Faster-than-light means of travel and communications throughout the galaxy

DATAPOINT: Originally ships navigated hyperspace by means of hyperspace beacons, but on-board navicomputers later replaced these.

SNAPSHOT: Hyperspace is an alternate dimension or state of reality reached when something travels faster than light, essentially moving from a baryonic to a tachyonic state. The Republic set up a faster-than-light communications system known as the HoloNet via hyperspace, and starships with hyperdrives regularly made the jump to hyperspace to be able to travel huge interstellar distances at speeds far faster than the speed of light. Without hyperspace technology, the Republic and the Empire that followed it would be much smaller enterprises, relegated to a fraction of their current space.

SUBSPACE

OCCUPATION: Faster-than-light communications medium

DATAPOINT: Life forms that inhabit subspace are encountered in the *Star Trek: The Next Generation* episode "Schisms."

SNAPSHOT: Subspace is an alternate version of normal space in which the standard laws of physics do not apply. It's possible to communicate almost instantaneously via subspace over huge interstellar distances, given enough relay stations for the signal. A Warp drive manages to exceed the speed of light by placing its ship in a subspace bubble, and transporters work by a similar procedure, sending items through subspace from one location to another.

WHO'D WIN?

Han Solo grins as he sits in the *Millennium Falcon,* which orbits around Earth alongside the *Enterprise (NCC-1701-B).* "You want to race for *what?*" he says.

"The old Earth phrase is 'for pinks,'" says Captain Kirk. "We race, and the winner of the race gets the loser's ship."

"Seriously?" Han shakes his head in disbelief. "And how far are we going?"

"Just to Pluto. Should take about half an hour."

Han checks his navicomputer. "All right," he says. "You're on."

"On my mark then. Ready? Set? Go!"

The *Enterprise* zips out of the Solar System at maximum Warp.

"Got those coordinates punched in yet, Chewie?"

The Wookiee growls at Solo, who smiles at him. "All right then, let's hit it."

The *Millennium Falcon* enters hyperspace.

When the *Enterprise* drops out of Warp, the *Millennium Falcon* sits in orbit around Pluto, and Solo has his boots up on the *Falcon*'s console. "What took you guys so long?" he asks. "I'm looking forward to checking out my new ship!"

RESULT: Hyperspace travel is insanely faster than Warp travel. Star Wars wins.

MEDICAL SCIENCE

When the heroes get banged up, they need to get back on their feet as fast as they can. You might not normally think of this as an issue of time and space, but it can be for the competitors involved. Medical attention doesn't get much coverage in the Star Wars films outside of the sickbay in the Rebel base on Hoth and a single spaceship in which Luke gets a new hand. It's all over Star Trek, of course, but one of the most interesting implementations is on *Voyager*, on which a hologram handles the doctoring duties.

How would they fare against each other?

THE *REDEMPTION* VS. THE DOCTOR

THE *REDEMPTION*

OCCUPATION: Medical frigate

DATAPOINT: The *Redemption* is the site of Luke's bionic clinic at the end of *Star Wars: The Empire Strikes Back.*

SNAPSHOT: The *Redemption* is the only medical frigate shown in the Star Wars films. It's a huge facility, an entire starship dedicated to providing medical care to Rebel forces harmed during the Galactic Civil War. It features many medical robots and full-immersion bacta tanks, not to mention amazing views.

THE DOCTOR

OCCUPATION: Emergency medical hologram, physician

DATAPOINT: Although early episodes of *Star Trek: Voyager* stress the Doctor's limitations, he gets an "upgrade" in the *Voyager* episode "Message in a Bottle."

SNAPSHOT: The Doctor is an emergency medical hologram programmed to serve a Federation starship in the absence of any other qualified physicians. When *Voyager* lost its entire medical staff thousands of light-years from home, the Doctor was pressed into service as the ship's full-time doctor. His adaptive programming means that he is able to learn and grow not only as a physician but also as a sentient being.

WHO'D WIN?

The *Redemption* is the equivalent of a huge, state-of-the art hospital facility capable of working on hundreds of patients at once. It's like the Mayo Clinic writ large.

The Doctor, on the other hand, is the embodiment of every bit of human medical knowledge garnered to date, uploaded and synthesized into a single program that does not miss diagnoses or make mistakes. Many of the medical droids on *Redemption* offer similar abilities, but none of them are capable of offering counseling services, as the Doctor can.

The key difference, though, is that the Doctor is right there on the ship—and can be installed, in theory, on any ship with similar holographic abilities in its sickbay. If you're hurt in a battle against the Empire, you have to hope that any nearby medics can stabilize you and keep you that way long enough for you to make it to the *Redemption*.

RESULT: Tough call, but give this one to the Doctor. There's nothing like having the medical staff you need on board.

PAST AND FUTURE

The past influences the present, and—at least in the case of Star Trek—the future has been known to influence the present as well. This reminds us not only that we have a history and a heritage of which we're a part, but also that our actions have meaningful ramifications that will affect people and events in the future. Both Star Wars and Star Trek deal with these issues in different but important ways.

THE OLD REPUBLIC VS. THE TEMPORAL COLD WAR

THE OLD REPUBLIC

OCCUPATION: Providing context for everything that happens in Star Wars films and TV shows

DATAPOINT: The Old Republic was founded 25,000 years before the Battle of Yavin, the conflict in which Luke Skywalker destroyed the Death Star.

SNAPSHOT: It's the time of *Star Wars: The Old Republic*, the new massively multiplayer online role-playing game (MMORPG) from Bioware set in the distant past of the Star Wars universe. Jedi of the Republic roam the galaxy in large numbers, opposed on many fronts by their ancient foes, the Dark Jedi of the Sith Empire. It is a time of epic conflict and dark intrigue, filled with possibilities for adventure.

THE TEMPORAL COLD WAR

OCCUPATION: Messing with the past to ensure a vision of the future

DATAPOINT: The first mention of the Temporal Cold War came in the *Star Trek: Enterprise* pilot episode "Broken Bow."

SNAPSHOT: In the far future, organizations in a number of different eras invent means of traveling freely through time and space. In the twenty-second century, Captain Archer becomes embroiled in a Temporal Cold War heating up among factions hailing from the twenty-first, twenty-eighth, twenty-ninth, and thirty-first centuries. This eventually forces the *Enterprise* to travel back to 1944 to stop the alien leader Vosk (a Na'kuhl from the twenty-ninth century) from initiating an all-out Temporal War.

WHO'D WIN?

Frustrated by his defeats, an alternate timeline version of Vosk decides to go farther and farther back into the past until he finally arrives at the time of the Old Republic. Once there, he strikes an alliance with the Sith Emperor to ensure the success of his efforts to destroy the Jedi. The *Enterprise (NX-01)* manages to make it back to the same time, though, and stops Vosk's efforts once again.

This time, the Sith Emperor takes control of Vosk's technology and goes all the way back to the beginning of sentient life in the galaxy. He finds the planets from which it all started, and he nukes them from orbit to make sure nothing on them can survive.

The resultant time paradox means that Vosk could never have existed to travel back so far in time to give the Sith Emperor the ability to travel even farther back and destroy all traces of the civilization that led to the existence of Vosk, the Sith Emperor, and time travel in the first place.

Time unravels. The end. But can you have an end if there was never a beginning?

RESULT: The Temporal Cold War wins just by making my head hurt enough I can't think about it any more.

OUR RUNNING TALLY

Time and Space

	SAGA THIS CHAPTER	RUNNING TALLY
Star Wars	3	34
Star Trek	2	33
Ties	0	3

Star Wars muscles out a small advantage here, giving it the lead once more. The fact that Star Wars takes up an entire galaxy, while Star Trek concentrates mostly on a single quadrant, might have played into this.

PART IV

SOCIETY
AND
CULTURE

Think of this as your citizenship test for either the Galactic Empire or the United Federation of Planets—a quiz on government.

1. **Before he became Emperor of the Galactic Empire, Palpatine's job was:**
   A. Jedi knight
   B. Chancellor of the Galactic Republic
   C. Smuggler
   D. King of Coruscant

2. **For currency, the Ferengi use:**
   A. Gold
   B. Dilithium crystals
   C. Gold-pressed latinum
   D. Dollars

3. **The fluid used to heal people in Star Wars is called:**
   A. Bacta
   B. Bactine
   C. Pennicillia
   D. Borax

4. **The first Emperor of the Klingon Empire was called:**
   A. Worf
   B. General Chang
   C. Kahless
   D. Kruge

5. **During *Star Wars: The Phantom Menace*, the money most commonly used on Tatooine was called:**
   A. Wupiupi
   B. Credits
   C. Bucs
   D. Crowns

6. **The Klingon and Vulcan languages were first created by:**
   A. Gene Roddenberry
   B. Majel Barrett-Roddenberry
   C. Leonard Nimoy
   D. James Doohan

Answers: 1. B, 2. C, 3. A, 4. C, 5. A, 6. D

CHAPTER 15

GOVERNMENT
The Man's Always with Us

Like it or not, government affects everyone in modern society, whether they care about politics or not. The same is true in both Star Wars and Star Trek. While the stories told in each saga boil down to the actions of individuals and teams, they're spun against and often inspired by the backdrop of galactic politics, which frames the larger contexts in which they take place.

Even in science fiction, there's just no escape from politics.

THE BENEVOLENT GOVERNMENTS
Each saga has its own version of the good government, the organization that's run by—or at least joined by—the heroes we're rooting for. We don't often get a good look at the internal politics of these organizations and have a chance to examine exactly how good they really are. We just know that they're clearly better than their murderous and oppressive alternatives.

THE GALACTIC REPUBLIC VS. THE UNITED FEDERATION OF PLANETS

THE GALACTIC REPUBLIC

OCCUPATION: Benevolent government of the galaxy

DATAPOINT: The Old Republic, as it was later known, ruled the galaxy for more than 25,000 years until the events that began in *Star Wars: The Phantom Menace.*

SNAPSHOT: According to the Expanded Universe material, the Galactic Republic had governed the galaxy for more than 25,000 years by the time Senator Palpatine of Naboo secretly launched his bid for power by backing a Separatist movement designed to terrify the Senate into giving ultimate power to him. Over the course of those twenty-five millennia, the Republic waxed and waned, but it never fell, not even in its battles against the Sith Empire. Today, though, the Republic has become encrusted with inside politics and petty bureaucrats and is ripe for a fall.

THE UNITED FEDERATION OF PLANETS

OCCUPATION: Governing an alliance of planets in the galaxy's Alpha Quadrant

DATAPOINT: The Federation is governed by a charter that features the Prime Directive as one of its most important elements.

SNAPSHOT: The United Federation of Planets—often just called the Federation—governs around 150 planets united under a common banner. Four founding species—Andorians, Vulcans, Tellarites, and Humans—established the UFP in 2161. While a peaceful union, it came into conflict with the Klingon Empire and the Romulan Star Empire, and many worlds joined the Federation as a bulwark against invasion by the other great powers in the galaxy. Today, having successfully fended off the Dominion invasion from the Delta Quadrant, the Federation is stronger than ever and has even developed decent relations between both the Romulans and the Klingons.

WHO'D WIN?

Rather than invent a new scourge of the Republic in the Confederacy of Independent Systems, Palpatine decides to instigate a war with the Federation, believing that the conflict will bind the Galactic Senate to him better than any conflict from within. Despite his best efforts, though, the Federation stymies his attempts again and again, steadfastly refusing to attack until they have a proper chance to investigate any of the terrorist attacks that Palpatine's agents have committed, trying to blame them on the Jedi. They just don't seem to want to go to war unless they're invaded.

Palpatine switches tactics then. His agents blow up a portion of the Senate and plant evidence that the culprits could only have come from the Federation. He then whips the Senate up into a fury and persuades the senators to proclaim war on the Federation. Calmer heads inside the Jedi Order try to investigate the disaster, but Palpatine frames them as traitors who helped the Federation execute its horrible attack.

The *Enterprise* joins up with the Jedi in an effort to clear both the Jedi and the Federation of any culpability in the attack. Can even Palpatine's lies hope to hold against such an alliance?

RESULT: While the Federation is the smaller organization, it's also the most mature and level-headed of the two. They get the win for being the better government.

MONEY

It's said that money makes the world go around, and that's as true in the Star Wars universe as anywhere. The saying seems to have gone out of fashion inside the Federation, though, which has no official currency. Because of replicators, they claim not to need it, but can that really be true?

CREDITS VS. FEDERATION ECONOMICS

CREDITS

OCCUPATION: A source of currency accepted across the galaxy

DATAPOINT: Obi-Wan uses credits to book passage on the *Millennium Falcon* in *Star Wars: A New Hope.*

SNAPSHOT: The Galactic Standard Credit has been the legal tender of the Republic since the days of its founding. Despite that, it's not universally accepted everywhere, particularly in backwater worlds far from the influence of Coruscant. Times change, though, and the Imperial credit—which replaced the Republic credit—is widely accepted throughout the galaxy again.

FEDERATION ECONOMICS

OCCUPATION: A means of making things happen without money as an incentive

DATAPOINT: Gold-pressed latinum serves as currency aboard Deep Space Nine.

SNAPSHOT: With the advent of replicator technology and the means to power it, the Federation eliminated all need in its population. Everyone is fed, housed, and clothed, and there is no need for currency to pay for such things. People work for the betterment of themselves and the Federation and don't concern themselves much with material things. Of course, this isn't true of the other civilizations in the galaxy, and for that reason the Federation government keeps a stock of currency it can use to trade with other governments should the need arise. Mostly, though, the Federation prefers to barter goods and services and negotiates such deals with outsiders on a case-by-case basis.

WHO'D WIN?

Han Solo sits down in Captain Sisko's office on Deep Space Nine. "So," Sisko says, "Odo tells me you're in a bind."

"You could say that. We have a price on our head, and we need to pay it off."

Sisko raises an eyebrow. "So how can we help?"

"You know the people here. I'm a good captain with a great ship. I can cross the entire galaxy in less than a week."

"Really?"

"Really," Solo says, ignoring the fact that Sisko clearly doesn't believe him. "All I need is a high-paying job fast. Then I can get Jabba his money."

Sisko shrugs. "I'm afraid I can't help you. We don't use money."

"I'm sorry, what did you just say?"

"We don't use money. If we need something we just replicate it."

"Replicate."

"Computer: Raktajino, hot."

A steaming mug of Klingon coffee appears in the replicator. Sisko picks it up, smells it, smiles, and takes a sip. "Would you like anything?"

"You bet," Solo says as he pulls an Imperial credit from his pocket. "Can you replicate this?"

RESULT: Replicators triumph over credits.

MERCHANTS

Despite the rise of the replicator, capitalism is alive and well in both Star Wars and Star Trek. Both galaxies feature merchants who make their living moving goods from one place to another, buying them at low costs and selling them at high prices. The freedom of the Trade Alliance to do this without taxation was one of the causes of the rise of the Separatist Movement. It's also the basis of the entire society of the Ferengi Alliance.

TRADE FEDERATION VS. FERENGI ALLIANCE

TRADE FEDERATION

OCCUPATION: Selling goods throughout the galaxy, starting wars

DATAPOINT: After the triumph of the Galactic Empire, the Trade Federation was dissolved and its functions imperialized.

SNAPSHOT: The Trade Federation has long been one of the most powerful guilds in the galaxy. Representing the interests of many powerful businesses, it lobbied on its members' behalf to the Galactic Senate, and it even helped establish negotiations with the Senate over controversial taxation plans. At the moment, the Trade Federation—under the leadership of the Neimoidian Nute Gunray—is preparing for an armed conflict with the Republic over its insistence on placing taxes on the Trade Federation's members.

THE FERENGI ALLIANCE

OCCUPATION: Making money any—and every—way it knows how

DATAPOINT: The Ferengi, often featured in *Star Trek: Deep Space Nine*, made their first offer in the *Star Trek: The Next Generation* episode "The Last Outpost."

SNAPSHOT: To the citizens of the Ferengi Alliance, only one thing in life really matters: money. It is the yardstick by which they measure their importance, and the wisdom they've accrued about how best to gather it is the basis of their oft-quoted Rules of Acquisition. As the First Rule states, "Once you have their money, never give it back."

WHO'D WIN?

"I'm sure we can come to an arrangement," Grand Nagus Zek says to Nute Gunray, Viceroy of the Trade Federation.

"I'm not so sure about that," says Gunray. "You have invaded our territory and are trying to steal our customers and ruin our businesses. This will not be tolerated!"

"Now, now, Mr. Gunray, surely you can see how our interests might become aligned. You have things to sell. We have people back home who I'm sure would love to buy them. And the same system would work in reverse. It's a simple import-export business arrangement. What could be easier?"

"I could order my droid army to destroy your ship and kill you all."

"Yes. Yes, you could, but think of the opportunity you'd be passing up here: opening up an entire new galaxy for exploitation. It's the chance of a lifetime!"

Gunray glares at Zek. Zek fidgets for a moment and then says, "Of course, we would have to establish head negotiators, who would, naturally, get a small percentage of every transaction that occurs between our two organizations. We will choose our own, as you might guess, and I would leave the selection of your soon-to-be-very-wealthy negotiator to you."

"You don't say," Gunray says as he strokes his chin.

"But I do, Mr. Gunray." A toothy smile spreads across Zek's face. "I most certainly do."

RESULT: The Ferengi get what they want: paid. They win.

REBEL LEADERS

Where there is a government, there is always opposition. In the case of a repressive regime like the Empire, the opposition can build until it gathers into an upstart Rebellion with hopes of changing the face of the galaxy. In the case of the Maquis, they are determined to protect their homes against the Cardassians, even if the Federation politicians have ceded that territory away in the interests of peace.

MON MOTHMA VS. THOMAS RIKER

MON MOTHMA

OCCUPATION: Former senator, current leader of the Rebel Alliance

DATAPOINT: Mon Mothma was played by British actress Caroline Blakiston in *Star Wars: Return of the Jedi.*

SNAPSHOT: Mon Mothma hails from the planet Chandrila, and at a young age she became a Senator in the Galactic Republic. As she watched Palpatine take over the government and later install himself as Emperor, she could not remain silent. She spoke openly in opposition to his assumption and abuse of power. When he finally tired of her and sent stormtroopers to arrest her, she escaped. After the death of Bail Organa during the destruction of Alderaan, she became the de facto leader of the Rebellion. At the moment, she's preparing for the biggest moment in the Rebellion's short history: the attempt to destroy the Death Star II.

THOMAS RIKER

OCCUPATION: Maquis leader, identical clone

DATAPOINT: Thomas Riker beamed into existence in the *Star Trek: The Next Generation* episode "Second Chances."

SNAPSHOT: Thomas Riker and Will Riker were once one person, but a transporter accident many years ago created two copies of Will—one of which was left marooned on a planet because no one knew he existed. After returning to Starfleet, the more impulsive Thomas became disgusted with the way the Federation had abandoned the human colonists who'd settled near Cardassian territory, and he decided to join the Maquis to work to protect the colonists, even if the Federation wouldn't.

WHO'D WIN?

Thomas Riker enters the safehouse in which Mon Mothma is hiding from the Empire: a private ship stationed at the spaceport in Mos Eisley. "I think perhaps we can help each other," he says. "We're both rebels of a sort. We both have good causes. Together we can be so much more effective than we could be alone."

"I don't see that," Mothma says. "We have our hands full with our own battles. After the destruction of the Death Star, we have the Empire teetering on the edge. We just need one more victory to topple it over."

"And we can help with that," says Riker, "right after you help us."

Mothma shakes her head. "We don't have time for that at the moment, I'm afraid. We're about to launch an attack against a key Imperial installation on Endor. We cannot distract ourselves from that. I'm sorry."

"No, I'm the one who's sorry." Riker pulls out a phaser. "If we can't have your support, I'm at least taking this ship."

RESULT: Riker may be ready to fight for what's right, but he's not above breaking a few rules to make it happen. Score a Pyrrhic victory for him here.

THE DESPOTS

In each saga, the heroes have fearsome foes they can fight against, but the struggles never seem more hopeless and valiant than when they face a massive, powerful, well-organized foe they can't at first even conceive how to defeat. That's where we separate the talkers from the doers and discover whether our heroes are out to save the galaxy or just their own skins.

So, what would happen if we pitched those staggering foes against each other?

THE GALACTIC EMPIRE VS. THE KLINGON EMPIRE

THE GALACTIC EMPIRE

OCCUPATION: Serving as the white-armored boot stomping the face of freedom

DATAPOINT: The Galactic Empire existed for nineteen years before the events depicted in *Star Wars: A New Hope*.

SNAPSHOT: The Galactic Empire under Emperor Palpatine is the most powerful government the galaxy has ever seen. The transformation of the clone army into the Emperor's stormtroopers gives the Empire a massive military power, and the destruction of the Jedi means that there's no one powerful enough to stand against them. Or so they think.

THE KLINGON EMPIRE

OCCUPATION: Keeping the ferocious Klingons focused on external threats rather than tearing themselves apart

DATAPOINT: The Klingon Empire finally stands on the brink of peace in the movie *Star Trek VI: The Undiscovered Country.*

SNAPSHOT: The Klingon Empire has reached a tipping point. It is near to achieving stability and peace. While wiser heads in the Empire have been looking forward to this eventuality, there are those within the Empire—some of whom are highly placed in the government—who would like nothing better than open war with the Federation instead. They see themselves as warriors for whom peace is nothing more than a time to let their blades grow dull.

WHO'D WIN?

The *Executor* pops out of hyperspace right next to Qo'noS, the Klingon homeworld. Taken by surprise, the Klingon High Council convenes an emergency meeting to speak with the representative from the massive ship who demands to speak with them over their viewscreen, an armored human who calls himself Darth Vader.

"What is it you want?" asks Chancellor Gorkon.

"I am here to welcome you as the newest subjects of the Galactic Empire," says Vader.

Gorkon stands up and slams his fist down on the table before him. "We Klingons pay tribute to no man!"

"The Emperor is no ordinary man, as you will soon see. He can be quite persuasive."

"You bring this message to your Emperor, lapdog! You, the coward who must hide his face behind his armor! We shall not be cowed by empty threats."

"You will find that the Empire's threats are never empty. If that is your answer, so be it. Make peace with whatever ridiculous gods you may have. Bombardment begins in thirty minutes."

Gorkon and his council toast each other with bloodwine and boast loudly of how they've called the armored one's bluff. They're still doing this when the *Executor's* first bombs strike the capital as it sets out to earn its name.

RESULT: The Klingons may be full of bombast, but they have absolutely no chance against the much bigger Galactic Empire.

OUR RUNNING TALLY

Government

	SAGA THIS CHAPTER	RUNNING TALLY
Star Wars	1	35
Star Trek	4	37
Ties	0	3

Star Wars seems to be more about politics than Star Trek, but most of its governments suck. The Republic is corrupt and inept, the Empire is evil, and the Rebels don't really have a government to speak of. Star Trek's more stable political landscape makes for more subtle effects and intrigue.

Even in the science-fiction universes of Star Wars and Star Trek, there seem to be higher powers. How much do you know about them?

1. **Those who follow the Dark Side of the Force are known as:**
   A. Mandalorians
   B. Gungans
   C. Midi-chlorians
   D. Sith

2. **The being who lived beyond the Great Barrier at the center of the Milky Way was:**
   A. God
   B. Q
   C. A powerful prisoner
   D. Sybok

3. **People who have the ability to manipulate the Force have in their blood a high count of:**
   A. Alcohol
   B. Midi-chlorians
   C. Paramecia
   D. White blood cells

4. **The Bajoran religion worshiped the creatures who lived in the Bajoran wormhole, known as:**
   A. The Olympians
   B. The Prophets
   C. The Founders
   D. The Galactic Priests

5. **In the era of the Star Wars films, the number of active Sith at any one time was:**
   A. One
   B. Two
   C. Thirteen
   D. Sixty-six

6. **The title of the top leader of the Bajoran religion was:**
   A. Kai
   B. Pope
   C. Torg
   D. Vedek

Answers: 1. D, 2. C, 3. B, 4. B, 5. B, 6. A

CHAPTER 16

RELIGION
A Higher Power

Everybody needs something to believe in—even if they just believe they'll have another drink. Some believe in themselves. Others believe in justice. Still others believe in power. Even in science fiction stories, though, there are people who believe in higher powers—and not just ones from the Q Continuum.

THE HIGHER POWERS

There are many different kinds of higher powers. Some worship a single god. Others respect a pantheon of gods, much as the Greeks and Romans did on ancient Earth. Their religion may require many things from them—some of which outsiders may see as odd—or it may only ask for simple respect for itself and for others.

THE FORCE VS. THE PROPHETS

THE FORCE

OCCUPATION: Binding everything together

DATAPOINT: The nature of the Force has been explored in spin-off books like *The Dharma of Star Wars* by Matthew Bortolin and *The Tao of Star Wars* by John M. Porter.

SNAPSHOT: As Obi-Wan Kenobi says, "The Force is what gives a Jedi his power. It's an energy field created by all living things. It surrounds us and penetrates us. It binds the galaxy together." It's not an entity to be worshiped so much as a way of understanding the universe that grants you some measure of control over it. The better you understand it, the more you can do. But not everyone can use or even detect the Force, and some are more powerful with it than others.

Much more.

THE PROPHETS

OCCUPATION: Communicating with the people of Bajor

DATAPOINT: Commander Sisko is identified as an Emissary of the Prophets in the pilot episode of *Star Trek: Deep Space Nine*.

SNAPSHOT: The Prophets are an alien species that lives in the only known stable wormhole in the galaxy, one end of which sits near the planet Bajor. The Prophets have communicated with the Bajorans for 30,000 years, mostly through a series of nine orbs that the Bajorans have found on and around Bajor. The Prophets have little sense of linear time, and outside of the wormhole, they can only communicate by taking possession of someone's body and speaking through her or him.

WHO'D WIN?

Obi-Wan Kenobi's Force ghost enters the Bajoran wormhole to speak to the Prophets. "Hello," he says, "I am a seeker of truth, and I would like to hear more of yours."

One of the Prophets coalesces out of the luminescence inside the wormhole. He looks like Qui-Gon Jinn. "How can we help you?"

Obi-Wan closes his eyes and reaches out to them with his mind. "Just hold still for a moment. There . . . ah."

"Have you received the answers you seek?"

"I believe so," says Obi-Wan. "You are an alien species from another dimension, are you not? One only partly intersecting with this one at certain special angles."

"That is a viable way of looking at it."

"If you don't mind me asking, what do you do for your followers?"

"We provide guidance."

"As in 'guiding a torpedo into the center of a giant space station so you can save the galaxy'?"

"No."

"How about granting your followers powers like speed, acrobatics, levitation, that sort of thing?"

"Sorry, no. We don't really understand those things very well."

"Can you let one of them choke someone from across the room?" Obi-Wan asks.

"Why would we want to do that?"

Obi-Wan nods. "Thank you for your time."

Qui-Gon morphs into Luke Skywalker and gives Kenobi a confused look. "Time? What's that?"

Kenobi smiles. "As in, 'time I should be going.'"

RESULT: The Force kicks the Prophets' collective butt. Or it would, if Vader had gone in there instead of Obi-Wan.

THE POWER USERS

In action-packed science fiction, it's not enough to be able to tap into the power of a god. You've got to be able to use it. Some manage this better than others, of course, but let's see what happens when we pit two of the biggest mystical guns in each universe against each other.

THE JEDI COUNCIL VS. Q

THE JEDI COUNCIL

OCCUPATION: Overseeing the Jedi, talking too much

DATAPOINT: The High Council led the Jedi for almost 4,700 years before it was dissolved at the beginning of the Galactic Empire.

SNAPSHOT: The Jedi High Council is made up of a dozen of the most powerful and respected Jedi in the galaxy—which makes them arguably the most potent individuals in the Republic. As Jedi Masters, they could use all sorts of mystical powers, including the ability to deflect incoming blaster fire with a lightsaber, jump long distances, push and levitate large items with the Force, and sense disturbances in the Force. Before their fall, the High Council included such famed Jedi as Yoda, Mace Windu, Ki-Adi-Mundi, Kit Fisto, Shaak Ti, Obi-Wan Kenobi, and Anakin Skywalker. Despite their supposed wisdom, Palpatine fooled them all—right up until it was too late to stop him.

Q

OCCUPATION: Messing with/helping advance humanity

DATAPOINT: Q has appeared in three Star Trek TV series: *Star Trek: The Next Generation, Star Trek: Deep Space Nine,* and *Star Trek: Voyager.*

SNAPSHOT: Q is a member of the Q Continuum, a dimension in which everyone who exists is also a Q named Q. He has the power to alter reality instantaneously, at his merest whim. He is immortal, omniscient, and whimsical, and he often appears naïve, immature, and bored out of his mind. For reasons known only to himself, he's taken an interest in humanity and seems to have a special affinity for the most powerful captains in Starfleet.

WHO'D WIN?

Q appears in the center of the Jedi High Council's chambers atop the Jedi Temple on Coruscant. "Are you the best that your 'hokey religion' can offer?" he says.

"I sense great power in this one," Shaak Ti says.

"Great work there," Q says. "I'll bet my midi-chlorian count is off the chart. Except I don't have any of those. Did you just make those up?"

Mace Windu and Obi-Wan Kenobi stand up and put their hands on the hilts of their lightsabers. "Who are you, and what are you doing here?" Windu asks.

"Isn't that rich," says Q. "You think you can intimidate me. How hilarious!"

Anakin Skywalker leaps up, draws his lightsaber, and ignites it. "You won't threaten us."

"Oh, I'm not threatening you. If I wanted you dead, you'd be dead."

Anakin moves forward, his glowing blade before him. "I think you'd better leave."

"Or what?" Q reaches out and grabs Anakin's lightsaber by the blade. It does not harm him at all.

Anakin tries to pull his blade away, but Q will not let it budge. "What's the expression?" he asks. "Oh, yes. 'If you strike me down, I will only become more powerful,' right? Except I'm not sure just how that could happen."

RESULT: There's no contest here. Even the Jedi have nothing on Q.

RELIGIOUS LEADERS

It's hard to have a religion without adherents. The trouble is that whatever the religion is based around is usually too busy to deal with the daily duties of running a church. They leave that sort of drudgery to their religious leaders instead.

SHAAK TI VS. KAI WINN

SHAAK TI

OCCUPATION: Member of the Jedi High Council

DATAPOINT: Shaak Ti first wields a lightsaber in the movie *Star Wars: Attack of the Clones.*

SNAPSHOT: The Togruta female Shaak Ti is considered one of the greatest Jedi of her era, both for her wisdom and her skill with a lightsaber. She helped save Obi-Wan Kenobi, Anakin Skywalker, and Padmé Amidala on Geonosis, and she led a contingent of clone troopers during the Clone Wars. She has the respect of every Jedi on Coruscant.

KAI WINN ADAMI

OCCUPATION: Head of the Bajoran religion

DATAPOINT: The kai sermonizes for the first time in the *Star Trek: Deep Space Nine* episode "In the Hands of the Prophets."

SNAPSHOT: Kai Winn may be the leader of the Bajoran religion, but she's also a politically savvy and ambitious woman who uses her supposed piety as a weapon against those who would stand in her way. She has spent most of the last few years working against the Prophets' chosen Emissary, Captain Sisko, because she can't understand how or why they would choose an alien (non-Bajoran) for such a vital role. Despite this, Winn strictly maintains her appearance as a staunch supporter of both the Emissary and the Prophets—especially in public.

WHO'D WIN?

Kai Winn walks up to Shaak Ti on the Promenade of Deep Space Nine and accosts her. "What are you doing here?" she says. "I've heard of your kind and your heretical religion. You are not wanted here."

"I do not understand," Ti says, maintaining her perfect composure.

"Here on Bajor—in Bajoran space—we worship the Prophets, not some strange, unseen 'Force' that operates in another part of the galaxy. We don't want you disrupting things here."

"I don't wish to be of any trouble to you."

"Then leave."

"But neither will I be bullied," the Jedi responds. "You will step back and let me proceed on my way."

"Or?"

"Or I will show you how my lightsaber works, and it will show you the most direct way to meet your Prophets—in your afterlife."

The two glare at each other for a long moment. Winn's stony facade breaks first. With a snooty *humph,* she turns and walks away, hoping that anyone in the area who sees her will still think she won their argument.

RESULT: Shaak Ti is happy to beat Kai Winn in her favorite way: without having to kill her.

THE SPIRITUALISTS

Not every religious person reveres a god. Some are content to simply explore the magic of the natural world and contemplate their ever-changing part in it. These people are more in tune with the world around them and understand it on a deeper level than most.

LOGRAY VS. CHAKOTAY

LOGRAY

OCCUPATION: Ewok shaman

DATAPOINT: Logray gives the ewoks Wicket and Kneesaa magical powder in the children's book *Star Wars: Return of the Jedi: How the Ewoks Saved the Trees* by James Howe.

SNAPSHOT: Logray is the shaman of the tribe of Ewoks that Princess Leia Organa befriends in the forests of Endor. The tribe's territory encompasses the Imperial shield-projection installation that protects the Death Star II while it's still under construction. Logray is a bit of a bully. He enjoys his position in the tribe, and he is willing to abuse what power it gives him so that he might hold on to it.

CHAKOTAY

OCCUPATION: First officer of the USS *Voyager*

DATAPOINT: Chakotay and Seven of Nine are married in the alternate reality of the *Star Trek: Voyager* series finale "Endgame."

SNAPSHOT: For many years, Chakotay ignored his heritage as a Mayan Native American. Instead of following in his father's spiritual footsteps, he joined Starfleet and put all that behind him. After the Cardassians killed his father, though, he joined the Maquis to fight them in his father's name. Now back with Starfleet, Chakotay is making a real effort to reconnect with his spiritual heritage, even going on vision quests during which he can speak with his father's spirit.

WHO'D WIN?

Chakotay finds himself wandering through a strange forest, and he nearly trips over what he first thinks is a teddy bear someone left in his way. The bear turns out to be an Ewok named Logray, who is not happy about the much bigger human almost crushing him.

Logray brings out a spear and grunts at Chakotay, "Watch where you're going!"

Chakotay puts up his hands. "I'm not here to hurt you. But I wouldn't mind talking for a bit."

"I have nothing to say to outsiders. Your kind only uses us for target practice."

"I'm not like the others," Chakotay says. "Honest."

"Do you have any food?"

"Nothing I can give you."

"Then you are as worthless to me as the rest of my tribe." Logray puts the tip of his spear against Chakotay's chest. "I will kill you and bring your corpse back to my tribe as proof of the favor the world gives me."

Chakotay smiles down at the Ewok. "No," he says, "I don't think you will."

"Why not?"

"Because this is my vision quest, not yours," Chakotay says. "And I'm afraid it's over."

And with that, he gently fades away.

RESULT: Chakotay is a true spiritualist, while Logray is just a bully. Chakotay wins.

THE WRONG RELIGIONS

Every religion seems to think its members are the chosen of the gods, the ones who will find all sorts of favors from the world, just as long as they remain faithful worshipers. Of course, they can't all be right. What if we took the two "wrongest" sets of adherents and pitted them against each other?

THE SITH VS. THE WAY OF THE WARRIOR

THE SITH

OCCUPATION: Thorn in the Jedis' collective side

DATAPOINT: Their golden age was recounted in the Dark Horse Comics series *Star Wars: Tales of the Jedi: The Golden Age of the Sith*, written by Kevin J. Anderson.

SNAPSHOT: At one point, the Sith Empire ruled over a good chunk of the universe, but those days are long since gone. Today, there are only ever two official Sith Lords in the entire galaxy, the apprentice and the master. This system has helped hone the remaining Sith into some of the most dangerous people in the galaxy.

THE WAY OF THE WARRIOR

OCCUPATION: Keeping the Klingons courageous and honorable

DATAPOINT: This philosophy is expounded in the *Star Trek: Voyager* episode "Barge of the Dead."

SNAPSHOT: In the Klingon religion, the first Klingons killed their gods soon after the gods created them. In revenge, the one god who escaped, Fek'lhr, now guards the gates of Gre'thor, the place to which disgraced Klingons go after they die. This nasty and violent version of Hell gives the Klingons every reason they need to be the best Klingons they can be: strong, courageous, honorable, and victorious.

WHO'D WIN?

Darth Maul enters a dark room filled with Klingons who are holding a wake for a departed friend killed in battle. Kurn, Worf's brother, steps up to Maul and demands to know who this stranger might be. Maul says nothing of course.

"Who sent you?" Nothing.

"Why are you here?"

In response, Maul draws his lightsaber and ignites it on both ends. The Klingons roar in approval.

"Fek'lhr has sent us a test! Let us kill this stranger and dance on his corpse tonight!"

With that, the Klingons throw down their drinks, snatch up their bat'leths, and rush Darth Maul. The Sith Lord's weapon moves like a blur, downing one Klingon after another, sometimes two or three at a time. The hum of the lightsaber along with the chorus of screams make a song that would awaken Fek'lhr and make him grin. When it is over, only Kurn remains, the one Klingon that Darth Maul has spared—for now.

As Maul leaves, Kurn knows exactly why he's been allowed to live: to tell the story of Maul so that his own legend might grow.

RESULT: Darth Maul dances on the Klingons' bumpy heads.

OUR RUNNING TALLY

Religion

	SAGA THIS CHAPTER	RUNNING TALLY
Star Wars	3	38
Star Trek	2	39
Ties	0	3

Star Wars pulls out the advantage here. You might think it would have taken more of the contest because so much of the franchise depends on the Force, but Star Trek really started exploring religion in the later series, particularly *Deep Space Nine*.

The ancient traditions of the Star Wars universe, and the rich future history of Star Trek, are unique cultures all their own. How much do you know about their peculiar art forms?

1. **The band that played at Jabba's palace was named after its keyboard player:**
   A. Max Rebo
   B. Mara Jade
   C. Sy Snootles
   D. Joh Yowza

2. **Bloodwine is a potent drink created by the:**
   A. Romulans
   B. Talaxians
   C. Andorians
   D. Klingons

3. **The diner at which Obi-Wan Kenobi ate in *Star Wars: Attack of the Clones* was called:**
   A. Dex's Diner
   B. The Full Moon
   C. The Mos Eisley Cantina
   D. Ten Forward

4. **The sexual practice on the planet Risa that killed Curzon Dax was called:**
   A. Jamaharon
   B. The Unification
   C. The Secret Pleasure
   D. Kamasutrinos

5. **After meeting Luke on Dagobah, Yoda feeds him:**
   A. Iron rations
   B. A candy bar
   C. Bantha cheese
   D. Rootleaf stew

6. **Commander William Riker often relaxed by playing the:**
   A. Fool
   B. Guitar
   C. Trombone
   D. Violin

Answers: 1. A, 2. D, 3. A, 4. A, 5. D, 6. C

CHAPTER 17

CULTURE
It Makes Life Worth Living

Galactic civilizations are known for more than just governments. Not everything is about war, diplomacy, or prayers. There's also the swirling clash of myriad cultures, each of which has its own kinds of art, labor, music, food, drinks, languages, and traditions—the heart and soul of galaxy-spanning cultures.

THE THEME SONGS

Both Star Wars and Star Trek are known for their classic theme songs. Though they have changed some over the years, most fans of science fiction can identify them in the opening bars. Some can even hum along by heart.

"MAIN TITLE FROM *STAR WARS*" VS. "THEME FROM *STAR TREK*"

"MAIN TITLE FROM *STAR WARS*"

OCCUPATION: Getting things started

DATAPOINT: The main title was performed by the London Symphony Orchestra.

SNAPSHOT: Legendary composer John Williams scored each of the Star Wars films, and he filled every one of them with memorable movements like "The Imperial March," which plays when Darth Vader comes on the screen. His most famous work is probably the soaring strains of the "Main Title from *Star Wars*," one of the most majestic and inspiring works of symphonic music recorded in the twentieth century.

"THEME FROM *STAR TREK*"

OCCUPATION: Rolling with the credits

DATAPOINT: The music ramps up right after ". . . to boldly go where no man has gone before."

SNAPSHOT: "Theme from *Star Trek*" played as the main and ending credits rolled during *Star Trek: The Original Series.* Though the music was written by Alexander Courage for the TV show, Gene Roddenberry reportedly wrote lyrics for it as well. They were never recorded for the show, and it's said that Roddenberry only wrote them so he could claim half the royalties for the song.

WHO'D WIN?

"Main Title from *Star Wars*" won several awards in 1977, the year the first Star Wars film debuted. These included an Oscar, a Saturn, a BAFTA Award, a Golden Globe, and a Grammy. To this day, the music for *Star Wars: A New Hope* remains the bestselling original score ever released.

While "Theme from *Star Trek*" never won any awards, it remains a well-known piece of music and a touchstone for Trekkies everywhere. A number of different versions were used during the original series, some of which had electronic instruments or a woman's voice singing a wordless tune over the rest of the music. In all cases, William Shatner delivered his famous monologue over the opening strains, starting with "Space, the final frontier."

If you put the two of them in a room and had them duke it out, though, it seems pretty clear who'd win.

RESULT: "Main Title from *Star Wars*" by John Williams. The London Symphony Orchestra nails it.

THE OUTSIDERS

Even in a galaxy filled with a staggering amount of variety, some characters just don't seem to fit in. They stand out from the crowd even when they're standing still, and when they open their mouths or move into action, they take over the screen. Let's take a couple such characters from very different angles and see how they do together.

SAVAGE OPRESS VS. GUINAN

SAVAGE OPRESS

OCCUPATION: Darth Tyrannus's latest apprentice

DATAPOINT: Savage Opress was summoned to class for the first time in the *Star Wars: The Clone Wars* episode "Monster."

SNAPSHOT: Savage Opress is the latest in a line of Dark Acolytes trained by Darth Tyrannus (Count Dooku) to help lead the Separatists' droid army under his command. When Asajj Ventress left his forces, she arranged for the Nightsisters to take a Zabrak male (perhaps related to Darth Maul) and transform him into a killing machine that could take her place at Dooku's side. Savage Opress quickly proved his worth, earning Dooku's acceptance.

GUINAN

OCCUPATION: Bartender

DATAPOINT: Ten Forward is under new management starting in the *Star Trek: The Next Generation* episode "The Child."

SNAPSHOT: Guinan may look human, but she's actually an El-Aurian who is well over 300 years old and possibly was the first alien to ever spend time on Earth. She came aboard the *Enterprise* to serve as the bartender in Ten Forward at the request of Captain Picard, whom she's known for many years. Though she's been married twenty-three times and has many children, she seems to be currently unattached and enjoys living on the *Enterprise.*

WHO'D WIN?

Savage Opress enters Ten Forward, hunting for someone. It's late at night, and Guinan is the only one there.

"Come on in," she says to him. "I've been expecting you."

Opress isn't impressed. He strides up to her and ignites his double-bladed lightsaber.

She rolls her eyes at his attempt to intimidate her. "Put that thing away before you hurt yourself, would you? You're not here for me, so let's just talk."

Opress takes the measure of the woman and then grunts and turns his lightsaber off. Guinan smiles and fixes him a drink.

"Now," she says. "I don't know much about you, but I do know that you're lost and a long way from home. If you want to get back, perhaps I can help you with that."

Opress nods cautiously.

"I can tell you that what you're looking for isn't here. You're just wasting your time on *Enterprise.*"

Opress scowls.

"The people who sent you here, they're just using you. They hope you'll overreact and do something stupid here, something that'll get you killed or—if you kill anyone here—bring the full weight of the Federation to bear on you."

Guinan leans forward. She can smell Opress's breath. "Now tell me," she says. "Does that sound like the kind of thing a smart guy like you should be interested in?"

RESULT: Guinan could talk the bark out of a dog. She wins this one.

FRIENDS, NEW AND OLD

The kind of friends you keep says a lot about you. They define where you're from, what you value, and whom you want to be. In the course of a long life, a lot of friends can move in and out of your life, no matter how long you might prefer to have them around. Let's examine a couple of the short-timers.

BIGGS DARKLIGHTER VS. TASHA YAR

BIGGS DARKLIGHTER

OCCUPATION: Rebel pilot

DATAPOINT: He gets his day in the sun in the Dark Horse Comic miniseries collected as *Star Wars: The Saga of Biggs Darklighter.*

SNAPSHOT: Biggs Darklighter is Luke Skywalker's childhood friend, the one who managed to get away from Tatooine and start exploring the galaxy while Luke was still stuck back on his aunt and uncle's moisture farm, hoping that his Uncle Owen's "just one more season" excuse for keeping him around would someday end. Biggs trained at the Imperial Academy to become an officer in the Emperor's army, but he later joined the Rebellion. He's happy to see Luke assigned to his own Red Squadron as they prepare to attempt to destroy the Death Star.

TASHA YAR

OCCUPATION: Security chief of the *Enterprise*

DATAPOINT: Tasha, who meets her untimely end in the *Star Trek: The Next Generation* episode "Skin of Evil," was played by Denise Crosby, granddaughter of crooner Bing Crosby.

SNAPSHOT: Orphaned at a young age, Tasha Yar had a horrible childhood, but she managed to make it into Starfleet Academy and turn her life around. Captain Picard personally recruited her for his security chief after watching her bravery in action. She is always willing to step up and defend her shipmates, no matter the consequences, and she is as faithful and stalwart a friend as you could ever hope to find. Unfortunately, she's a bit headstrong, which may not serve her well as security chief.

WHO'D WIN?

Tasha Yar steps into the Cantina in Mos Eisley. Biggs Darklighter spots her immediately and offers to buy her a drink.

"I'm on duty," she says.

"Then can I help you perform your duty?"

Tasha scans the bar over Darklighter's shoulder. "Perhaps," she says. "I'm looking for a friend of mine. He's dressed like me, dark skin, forehead ridges."

"Ah, yes." Darklighter grins. "The Wookiee's wrestling partner. He's recovering over there in the corner. A droid dressed like that tried to come in here a while ago. I'd wondered if he was looking for him too."

"He was," Yar says. She spots Worf and sees that he's all right, busy taking the edge off his humiliation with a fresh glass of bloodwine.

"Well," says Darklighter, "now that I've helped you out, I don't think we're strangers anymore. Can I still get you that drink?"

Yar smiles, more comfortable now that she's found Worf and knows he's okay. "Why not?" she says. "It's a short life, right?"

"Too short," Darklighter says with a wistful smile. "Far, far too short."

RESULT: Call this one a draw. They're already doomed anyhow.

ROGUES

Every culture has those who stand just outside of the mainstream, hunting for any angle they can use to their advantage. They may be thieves, schemers, criminals, or just less scrupled than most, but the best do it with style, class, and an honest desire to get rich without hurting anyone—or having to work too hard at it. Let's match up a couple of notable rogues and see how they fare against each other.

LANDO CALRISSIAN VS. THADIUN OKONA

LANDO CALRISSIAN

OCCUPATION: Administrator of Cloud City on the planet Bespin

DATAPOINT: Lando is the star of a trilogy of novels by L. Neil Smith: *Star Wars: The Lando Calrissian Adventures.*

SNAPSHOT: Lando Calrissian has always liked taking chances, even if that means breaking the law. His talent at the sabacc table has won and lost him fortunes—including the *Millennium Falcon*—and it even landed him his latest job: running Cloud City. Lando's hoping to take it easy and settle down here for a while. As long as he can keep himself out of the way of the Empire's scanners, it might just work out.

THADIUN OKONA

OCCUPATION: Captain of the starship *Erstwhile*, a private cargo carrier

DATAPOINT: As seen in the *Star Trek: The Next Generation* episode "The Outrageous Okona."

SNAPSHOT: Captain Thadiun Okona is a rogue, and he knows it. Hell, he enjoys it. With the *Erstwhile* at his beck and call, he can always leave the planet any time he attracts too much of the wrong kind of attention. He wouldn't call himself a smuggler, but maybe he doesn't ask as many questions as he could about the cargo and passengers he sometimes carries. But that's their business, not his, right?

WHO'D WIN?

Thadiun Okona disembarks from the *Erstwhile* on a landing platform in Cloud City and finds Lando Calrissian waiting there to greet him. "To what do I owe this honor?" Okona asks.

Calrissian smiles without humor. "I know who you are, Captain Okona. I've heard all about you. I'm hear to tell you that Cloud City doesn't need your kind here."

"Oh, really?" Okona grins at the attempted brush-off. "Is that because you're already filling that position yourself? That's right, I know all about you, too, Lando—and *my* kind? That's *your* kind you're insulting."

Calrissian grimaces. "Keep your voice down, will you? This is exactly why I came out here, so we could have this chat in private."

Okona looks around at the open platform hanging in the clouds. "You call this private?"

"Compared to inside, yes." Calrissian runs his tongue over his teeth. "Look, I just don't want any attention drawn here right now. I already have the Empire starting to breathe down my neck."

"You mean like, 'Hoo-paaah, hoo-paaah'? I hate it when Vader does that."

"So you see why you need to leave."

"Chewbacca says hi."

Calrissian freezes.

"Han does too. They have the most amazing stories about you."

Calrissian puts up his hands. "All right. All right, you got me." He turns and puts an arm around Okona's shoulders and starts escorting him into Cloud City. "Just keep all that to yourself, and you can stay the night."

"The week."

"All right, the week, but not a day more."

"Do you have anything in a luxury suite?"

"Don't push your luck."

RESULT: The well-traveled Okona takes this round.

WATERING HOLES

Most cultures have some kind of public gathering place: bars, taverns, longhouses, or whatever else you'd like to call them. Here you can have a seat, order a drink, and relax for a while before you have to get back to adventuring across the galaxy. The kind of watering holes they have tell you a lot about the people: who they are, what they like doing, and how much they're willing to pay to do it. Time to put a couple of the most famous bars in the galaxy up against each other to see how they fare.

MOS EISLEY CANTINA VS. QUARK'S BAR

MOS EISLEY CANTINA

OCCUPATION: A rough place with rough drinks for rough people

DATAPOINT: Mark Jonathan Davis created a parody of Barry Manilow's "Copacabana" titled "Star Wars Cantina," which was released in 1996.

SNAPSHOT: If the wretched hive of scum and villainy known as Mos Eisley has a beating heart, it's here in the Cantina—probably lying on the floor where it can get stepped on, or hooked up to a machine that keeps it pumping for the crowd's entertainment. All sorts of aliens wander through Mos Eisley, and the thirstiest and most dangerous ones get their drinks here as they listen to the best band on the planet. No droids allowed.

QUARK'S BAR

OCCUPATION: Lightening the pockets and bank accounts of customers and making sure they come back for more

DATAPOINT: The bar appeared in practically every single episode of *Star Trek: Deep Space Nine.*

SNAPSHOT: Quark ran his bar back when this space station was in Cardassian hands, and he runs it now that the Federation has taken over, too. He wanted to get out of it, but Captain Sisko cut him a deal too juicy to refuse, and business has been great. Quark serves food and drink of all kinds and runs a number of tables of games of chance. He also rents out holosuites by the hour. He's shady but honest in a Ferengi way, and if you need anything in this part of the galaxy, Quark's is where you go to get it—or find out where you can.

WHO'D WIN?

Quark enters the Cantina and scopes the place out as he works his way to the bar. Once he gets the bartender's attention, he orders a black hole. When the bartender returns with his drink, Quark says, "Can I ask you a question, friend?"

The bartender gives the Ferengi a curt nod that tells him to make it quick. Quark ignores that.

"How do you turn a profit in a place like this?" asks the Ferengi. "Oh, I know, there's plenty of people here, but that's what doesn't make sense. How do you get so many people into a dive like this? Where are the Dabo tables? Or the Dabo *girls?* How about the holosuites? I tell you, you're leaving money in people's pockets around here, my friend."

The bartender throws his rag over his shoulder and leans over the bar. "See these people here? I don't care who they are. I don't care who they killed, what they stole, or how many systems they have the death penalty in. They may not be able to sit down and drink anywhere else, but they're welcome here."

Across the bar, a lightsaber hums and flashes, and a violent man falls. His body goes one way, and his arm goes another.

"Plus," the bartender says, "most of them really enjoy our impromptu floor shows."

RESULT: Quark may not understand it, but the bartender knows his business. Chalk up a win for the lower-overhead Cantina.

OUR RUNNING TALLY

Culture

	SAGA THIS CHAPTER	RUNNING TALLY
Star Wars	2	40
Star Trek	2	41
Ties	1	4

The fact that both sagas tied here doesn't surprise me. Each has a vibrant culture that sings onscreen. Star Trek comes out of this chapter with a one-point edge. Will it last?

PART V

PREPARE FOR IMPACT

QUIZ 18

Test your business acumen with these questions concerning the realities behind the fantasies.

1. **As of 2010, *Star Wars: A New Hope* is the second-highest-grossing film of all time, adjusting for inflation. The first is:**
   A. *Avatar*
   B. *E. T.: The Extra-Terrestrial*
   C. *Titanic*
   D. *Gone with the Wind*

2. **The *Enterprise* headed out on a five-year mission in the original series. It lasted a total of how many seasons?**
   A. Three
   B. Seven
   C. One
   D. Five

3. **George Lucas created a special effects company to handle the effects for *Star Wars*. It's called:**
   A. Industrial Light and Magic
   B. Idea and Design Works
   C. Weta Workshop
   D. Star Warriors

4. **The highest-grossing *Star Trek* film, as of 2010, is:**
   A. *Star Trek: The Motion Picture*
   B. *Star Trek II: The Wrath of Khan*
   C. *Star Trek: Generations*
   D. *Star Trek (2009)*

5. **The number of real-life years between *Star Wars: Return of the Jedi* and *Star Wars: The Phantom Menace* was about:**
   A. Sixteen
   B. Twenty-four
   C. Twelve
   D. Twenty-one

6. ***Star Trek: The Next Generation, Star Trek: Deep Space Nine,* and *Star Trek: Voyager* are tied for the longest-running *Star Trek* series. They each ran:**
   A. Five seasons
   B. Six seasons
   C. Seven seasons
   D. Ten seasons

CHAPTER 18

FORTUNE AND GLORY
What All Adventurers Seek

We've witnessed pitched battles and friendlier encounters between sets of heroes, villains, and more from both universes. It's been a hell of a fun ride that's taken us all over two galaxies and back. Now it's time to come back to Earth and consider the impact that each of these enduring properties has had on a third universe: our own.

THE BATTLE OF THE BOX OFFICE

There's one measure of a saga that we can put down in hard numbers. It requires no opinions; it can be tallied up in Arabic numerals and then stared at with a cold eye. That is, of course, the measure of money.

STAR WARS VS. STAR TREK

STAR WARS

OCCUPATION: Box-office hits and licensing juggernaut

DATAPOINT: It is the third-highest-grossing film series ever, behind James Bond and Harry Potter.

SNAPSHOT: To date, the six Star Wars films and their various editions have grossed over $2.2 billion at the U.S. box office, $4.5 billion worldwide. A 2010 *Forbes* magazine article stated that Lucasfilm had also made over $20 billion in merchandising by producing or licensing everything from computer games to LEGO products to lunch boxes. That made George Lucas one of the wealthiest people in the world, with an estimated worth of $3.25 billion.

STAR TREK

OCCUPATION: Making money from science fiction fans, on screens of any size

DATAPOINT: The Star Trek franchise is currently owned by CBS.

SNAPSHOT: As of today, the Star Trek films have grossed just over $1 billion at the U.S. box office over the course of eleven installments. It's hard to guess at just how much money the franchise has made over the years—no one really has numbers for the advertising revenues and DVD sales for the various TV shows, for instance—but in 2006, MSNBC estimated Star Trek to have been worth over $4 billion total to Paramount, and that was before J.J. Abrams's new hit movie came along in 2009.

WHO'D WIN?

This really isn't much of a contest. While Star Trek has made a lot of money over the years, it stands in the shadow of Star Wars, which is widely regarded as the most successful entertainment property ever. Only Harry Potter even comes close. One huge reason for the success of Star Wars was the deal that George Lucas cut for the original film. He didn't get money up front, but he retained control over the final cut of the film, plus he kept the rights to any sequels and to all merchandise based on the film.

Back in 1977, 20th Century Fox probably thought this was a good deal and maybe believed they were taking advantage of a man desperate to have his movie made. Star Wars, of course, turned out to be a huge hit, and Lucas exploited those merchandising rights more thoroughly than anyone had ever managed before. In a sense, Star Wars created the modern merchandising industry that now brings us things like SpongeBob pajamas and Pokémon toothpaste. Brands now mean everything.

Star Trek had a lot of shows on TV, and many of them have been running in syndication around the world for decades. Still, it's hard to see how all of that money could add up to the extra $20 billion it would need to overtake Star Wars.

RESULT: Star Wars, in a landslide of credit chips.

CRITICAL ACCLAIM

You can't put a number on a fan's love. There's no tool you can properly calibrate to measure the passion with which someone cares about Star Wars or Star Trek. However, you can take a look at other things, like the number of awards and positive reviews a franchise has collected.

STAR WARS VS. STAR TREK

STAR WARS

OCCUPATION: Early critical darling

DATAPOINT: An Oscar winner since April 3, 1978.

SNAPSHOT: Though critics have not been as kind to the prequel films (Episodes I, II, and III), they loved the original trilogy

(Episodes IV, V, and VI). *Star Wars: A New Hope* was nominated for ten Academy Awards, and it won six of them, plus a special award for achievement in sound effects. In total, the Star Wars films have been nominated for twenty-two Oscars and won eight, plus three special achievement awards. The TV show *Star Wars: Clone Wars* also won three Emmys.

STAR TREK

OCCUPATION: Long-lived fan favorite

DATAPOINT: Star Trek's first Emmy win came in 1975 for, of all things, the Animated Series.

SNAPSHOT: The eleven Star Trek films have been nominated for fourteen Oscars. In 2010, *Star Trek (2009)* garnered four nominations, and it brought home the franchise's first-ever Oscar. It won for Best Makeup. The various Star Trek television series have earned an amazing 155 Emmy nominations, and they've won thirty-three in all.

WHO'D WIN?

As far as films go, this is a walk for Star Wars. Critics—and everyone else—especially loved *Star Wars: A New Hope*. As the freshness of the series wore off, the acclaim diminished, particularly for the prequels. However, it still gets far more love than Star Trek, which has had less than two-thirds of the nominations from nearly twice the number of films. Also the eight Oscar wins for Star Wars crushes Star Trek's single trophy.

When it comes to television, though, it's an entirely different story. Star Trek has racked up 155 Emmy nominations and thirty-three awards, while Star Wars has only brought home two trophies. That does mean that Star Wars has won every Emmy for which it's been nominated, but Star Trek still has more than sixteen times as many Emmys.

It's impressive that both franchises have done so well. The Oscars and Emmys often go to artier films and have a habit of looking down their noses at movies or shows that have had huge commercial success. In that sense, both franchises are huge winners.

RESULT: All things being equal, let's call this one a draw.

COMMUNICATIONS INFLUENCES

Thanks to cell phones, being in constant communication with anyone anywhere is no longer a dream of the far-flung future, but back when both sagas launched, such a notion was still science fiction. The idea that you could flip open a communicator and start talking with someone hundreds if not thousands of miles away felt impossible to people who still had to use rotary telephones attached to land lines. Both universes have influenced the way we talk with others. Let's see how.

DROID VS. FLIP PHONE

DROID

OCCUPATION: Android platform smartphone

DATAPOINT: The word *droid* is a registered trademark of Lucasfilm.

SNAPSHOT: In the fall of 2008, HTC shipped its Dream, the first smartphone to use Google's Android mobile operating system. Since then, a number of Motorola and HTC next-generation smartphones using Android have been released under the name Droid. To make this work, Lucasfilm licensed the name Droid to Verizon Wireless.

THE FLIP PHONE

OCCUPATION: Making you look like Captain Kirk when you call for a pizza

DATAPOINT: The first mobile phone, demonstrated in 1973, weighed 4.4 pounds.

SNAPSHOT: In 1996, Motorola released its StarTAC mobile phone, the first to use the clamshell design commonly known as the "flip phone." The devices look suspiciously like the communicator used in *Star Trek: The Original Series.* The only functional difference is that you might have to push a button or seven after you flip the phone open, but voice-activated dialing can even take care of that for you.

WHO'D WIN?

Once upon a time, way back at the turn of the century, the flip phone was the most popular cell phone style around. Motorola's RAZR line, for example, seemed to be everywhere. You just couldn't get away from it.

Then the smartphone came along. They started out with versions from Palm, then the BlackBerry got into the game. In 2007, with the release of the iPhone, Apple began to dominate the smartphone market.

Today, the once futuristic flip phones seem dated, and touchscreen smartphones are all the rage. (Ironically, the iPad, which some have called an overgrown iPhone, strongly resembles the PADDs found on *Star Trek: The Next Generation.*) Android phones, particularly the Droid series, are growing in popularity. As they ascend, fewer and fewer of us are able to flip open our phones anymore and say, "Kirk here."

RESULT: The Droid is a much cooler phone, but Star Trek does a better job of inspiring doable tech. Call this one a draw.

THE VIDEO GAMES

Both Star Wars and Star Trek have been the basis of a number of video games over the years. The first Star Trek game came out in

1971, and in 1973, *Empire*—an unlicensed game set in a *Star Trek*–like galaxy—became one of the first multiplayer action video games ever made. The first Star Wars video game was *Star Wars: The Empire Strikes Back*, which came out in 1982 for the Atari 2600. Loads of games have been released since and kept gamers' thumbs sore for decades. But which series has the best?

STAR WARS VIDEO GAMES VS. STAR TREK VIDEO GAMES

STAR WARS VIDEO GAMES

OCCUPATION: Letting gamers knock foes around with the Force

DATAPOINT: The first Star Wars video games were released on the Atari 2600 back in 1982.

SNAPSHOT: In less than thirty years, well over a hundred licensed video games have been based on Star Wars. Notables include the LEGO Star Wars series, the Star Wars: X-Wing series, *Star Wars: Dark Forces,* the Star Wars: Jedi Knight series, and *Star Wars: Knights of the Old Republic.* In 2003, the first Star Wars MMORPG—*Star Wars: Galaxies*—was released, and a brand-new one—*Star Wars: The Old Republic*—appears in 2011. Recently, we've seen other hit Star Wars titles like *Star Wars: Battlefront*, *Star Wars: Republic Commando*, and the Star Wars: The Force Unleashed series.

STAR TREK VIDEO GAMES

OCCUPATION: Giving people a reason to play on the computer since 1971

DATAPOINT: The first Star Trek video game was released in 1971 and was a text-only game.

SNAPSHOT: Star Trek video games have been around since the first one was programmed in BASIC in 1971, years after the original series had ended and even more years before *Star Trek: The Motion Picture* would jumpstart the franchise again. Standouts include *Star Trek: Armada* and *Star Trek: Voyager: Elite Force*. Arguments between Activision and Viacom meant no Star Trek games came out in the middle of the first decade of the twenty-first century, but they've since resumed with the games *Star Trek: D-A-C* and the MMORPG *Star Trek Online*.

WHO'D WIN?

The Star Wars video games have had a leg up on the Star Trek games for the past three decades for a few reasons. First, instead of having to base the games on the films, Star Wars game developers were able to tap into the entire Expanded Universe. This gave us critically acclaimed games like *Star Wars: Knights of the Old Republic*, widely regarded as one of the greatest video game RPGs of the past decade.

While Star Trek has amassed many different stories over its decades' worth of shows and films, there was often little room to breathe between these tales, making developing a game for the franchise more challenging. The fact that it often takes years to develop a decent game made it that much more difficult to be able to release a game that felt relevant to the ongoing shows, the storylines of which were being written at the same time.

Second, George Lucas didn't just license the games out. He also founded LucasArts, his own game development studio and game publisher. LucasArts made not only Star Wars games but many original games too. This cut down on approval problems and helped avoid the troubles that plagued the deal Paramount had with Activision.

RESULT: As a group, it's the Star Wars games for the win!

FANS

Both Star Wars and Star Trek have some of the most passionate fans on the planet. Countless people not only watch the shows and films but also read the books, play the games, wear the costumes, and sometimes even draw a good chunk of their personal identity from their love of their chosen saga. So, which fan base is stronger?

STAR WARS FANS VS. TREKKIES

STAR WARS FANS

OCCUPATION: Loving the Star Wars universe

DATAPOINT: Star Wars Celebration 2010 drew 32,000 fans.

SNAPSHOT: Star Wars has some of the most hardcore fans of any entertainment franchise. The members of the 501st Legion spend their nights making stormtrooper armor and their weekends wearing it. There have been seven massive Star Wars Celebration conventions over the past dozen years with up to 35,000 people attending over three days.

TREKKIES

OCCUPATION: Loving the Star Trek universe

DATAPOINT: Enterprising entrepreneurs have marketed a replica of the captain's chair from *Star Trek: The Original Series*. It comes complete with working lights and switches and even plays the "hailing frequencies" sound.

SNAPSHOT: Whether you call them Trekkies or Trekkers, Star Trek fans are among the most dedicated in the world. They love to dress up in costumes and debate the finer points of the franchise for endless hours. They appear at science fiction and pop culture conventions around the country and even have a series of conventions dedicated exclusively to their passion. These events have been going on fairly continuously since 1972. At one point in the early 1990s, there were more than 110 Star Trek conventions every year.

WHO'D WIN?

Star Trek fans have a head start of eleven years over Star Wars fans, but Lucas and his promotional team knew about science fiction and pop culture conventions too. They had teams attend three major conventions—the Western Regional Science Fiction Convention (Westercon), the San Diego Comic-Con (now Comic-Con International), and the World Science Fiction Convention (Worldcon)—in 1976, the year before *Star Wars: A New Hope* came out. They reached out directly to the fans because they knew that they would be the key to building buzz around the new film.

Both franchises have had continual presences at conventions since they started so many years ago. Many people are fans of both properties and regularly attend conventions dedicated to either. At numerous pop culture conventions, the stars and other professionals associated with both Star Wars and Star Trek share the convention hall with each other. Fans stand in line to meet and get autographs from them all.

RESULT: Both sets of fans are about as passionate as they can be. This one has to be a draw.

OUR RUNNING TALLY

Fortune and Glory

	SAGA THIS CHAPTER	RUNNING TALLY
Star Wars	2	42
Star Trek	0	41
Ties	3	7

When it comes to money and acclaim, Star Wars blows Star Trek away. Still, Star Trek does a fine job pulling out three ties here, the most in any chapter. Despite that, it's not enough to keep Star Wars from squeaking out a win.

We're almost there, but there are a few questions left to be answered. How big a fan of the series are you *really*?

1. ***Star Wars: A New Hope*** **was nominated for ten Oscars and—in addition to a Special Achievement Award for sound effects—won:**
   A. Six
   B. Ten
   C. Zero
   D. Four

2. ***Star Trek (2009)*** **won the first ever Academy Award for the series. The film was honored for:**
   A. Best Actor
   B. Best Makeup
   C. Best Director
   D. Best Special Effects

3. **The scores for all of the Star Wars films were written by:**
   A. Philip Glass
   B. John Williams
   C. Hans Zimmer
   D. Ennio Morricone

4. ***Hamlet*** **has actually been translated into:**
   A. Klingon
   B. Vulcan
   C. Romulan
   D. Borg

5. **The 501st Legion (named after the Imperial costuming organization) is also known as:**
   A. The Emperor's Children
   B. Coruscant's Pride
   C. Jedi Fodder
   D. Vader's Fist

6. **In 1996, Barbara Adams served as an alternate juror for a court trial while wearing a Starfleet uniform. The trial concerned:**
   A. The Menendez Brothers
   B. Elian Gonzalez
   C. Whitewater
   D. O. J. Simpson

Answers: 1. A, 2. B, 3. B, 4. A, 5. D, 6. C

CHAPTER 19

WHO WON?

All right. After eighteen chapters of various characters and elements from both Star Wars and Star Trek endlessly duking it out for our entertainment, it's time to declare the winner!

If you've been following along with the running tallies at the end of each chapter, you already know this, but let's make it official.

STAR WARS WINS!

THE POST-GAME ANALYSIS

Of course, it's never that simple. Let's take a look at that final tally.

The Final Tally

	SAGA GRAND TOTAL
Star Wars	42
Star Trek	41
Ties	7

Star Wars did, in fact, win, but it did so by the thinnest of margins. Its total beat Star Trek's by a single measly point.

How about we close it off with one more quiz?

Here's the twentieth and last set of questions designed to test your *Star Trek* and *Star Wars* knowledge. How have you done so far?

1. **The day job Gene Roddenberry gave up to become a writer for television was as a:**
   A. Fighter pilot   C. Police officer
   B. Science teacher   D. Preacher

2. **James Doohan, who plays the Scottish Montgomery Scott, is actually:**
   A. American   C. Welsh
   B. English   D. Canadian

3. **When he destroyed the Death Star, Luke Skywalker was flying:**
   A. An X-wing   C. The *Millennium Falcon*
   B. A Y-Wing   D. A Star Destroyer

4. **Lieutenant Deanna Troi was half human and half:**
   A. Klingon
   B. Vulcan
   C. Golian
   D. Betazoid

5. **George Lucas's first feature film was:**
   A. *American Graffiti*
   B. *THX 1138*
   C. *Star Wars: A New Hope*
   D. *Raiders of the Lost Ark*

6. **The captain of the first Earth ship to reach Warp 5—the *Enterprise* (NX-01)—was:**
   A. Jonathan Archer
   B. James T. Kirk
   C. Benjamin Sisko
   D. Wesley Crusher

Answers: 1. C, 2. D, 3. A, 4. D, 5. B, 6. A

CHAPTER 20

THE WAR ON TREK

Before you turn the final pages of this book, it's time for one last contest between the two universes. In this case, we saved the best for last.

What if the Empire invaded the Federation?

For this one, we're throwing out the Star Wars Vs. Star Trek bit. The good guys and the bad guys can cross franchise lines and join up with each other to do the most damage or good they can.

This isn't about which property is better than the other. It's the battle over the fate of both universes.

GOOD VS. EVIL

Having learned of the existence of the future galaxy in which Star Trek exists, the Emperor decides that it shall be his. As the glow from the triumph of establishing the Empire begins to fade, he knows that his subjects will eventually begin to turn against him—unless he can convince them that they need him, that he is the lesser evil.

This will take some doing, but it beats waiting around for Vader to finally man up and find the guts to try to kill him.

GOOD VS. EVIL

THE STAR WARS GALAXY

OCCUPATION: The rise, fall, and redemption of Anakin Skywalker, writ large

DATAPOINT: Ronald Reagan was annoyed when his missile defense system was labeled "Star Wars" by the media. But his assistant secretary of defense Richard Perle convinced him the name was complimentary.

SNAPSHOT: The Empire has just celebrated its twentieth anniversary, and the Emperor worries that he hasn't done enough to cement his power. With the destruction of the Death Star, he knows that others will finally see him as vulnerable, and that perception will make everything he hopes to accomplish more challenging. Even if he can somehow manage to keep Darth Vader cowed until the time comes for him to pass away from old age in a nice warm bed, Palpatine knows that the Rebels won't let him alone for that long. He needs to crush them or distract them—and distractions are so much easier.

THE STAR TREK GALAXY

OCCUPATION: Exploring the Final Frontier and learning more about ourselves as we go

DATAPOINT: In no TV episode or movie did Captain Kirk actually say the words "Beam me up, Scotty."

SNAPSHOT: The Federation has changed a lot since the days that Jonathan Archer blazed a trail into the wider galaxy aboard the first starship *Enterprise*. Former enemies, like the Klingons, are now trusted allies. Even the Romulans seem to be ready to make a strong and lasting peace. While it might seem impossible that the Federation could someday come to terms with the Dominion or the Borg, the fact that the Federation's former enemies are now becoming its partners makes anything seem possible—as long as good people work to make it happen.

WHO'D WIN?

The Emperor decides he needs to know more about the Star Trek galaxy, and now. To that end, he sends the still-in-progress Death Star II out on a mission to find allies among those strange new worlds—and set them up so that he can betray them.

Under Grand Moff Tarkin's leadership, the Death Star II works its way into the Delta Quadrant. There, the Imperial space station encounters the Borg. During a massive battle in which the Death Star II destroys several Borg cubes, a number of Borg soldiers manage to beam onto the space station and begin assimilating the Imperial soldiers they find there. Soon, the Death Star II belongs to the Borg.

One ship escapes from the Death Star II: the personal Lambda-class shuttle of Darth Vader. Evading the Borg's attempts to capture him, Vader makes his way back to the Star Wars galaxy. When he arrives, he goes straight to the Emperor to bring him the news.

Rather than kill Vader—as Vader might have done to anyone who had failed him so badly—Palpatine smiles. This is just the foe he needs to rally the entire galaxy around his banner.

The Emperor contacts the Rebellion's leaders and shows them the recordings Vader has made of the Borg. He tells them about the Death Star II and how much of a danger it is now that it has fallen into the wrong hands. He urges them to rally with him so that they may stand together against this horrible new evil.

The Rebels suspect a trick. They decide to send a ship out to confirm the Emperor's claims. They choose the *Millennium Falcon*, aboard which fly Han Solo, Luke Skywalker, Chewbacca, C-3PO, R2-D2, and Princess Leia Organa.

The *Falcon* makes it to the Delta Quadrant and discovers that Vader was telling the truth. Speaking with Neelix, Luke Skywalker learns that the Death Star II has been finished and has become a massive Borg Star, and it has left for the Gamma Quadrant.

The Borg Star moves deep into Dominion territory and launches an attack directly against the Founders' new homeworld. As the Borg are unable to assimilate the liquid forms of the Founders, Grand Borg Tarkin orders the destruction of their homeworld. In under a minute, the Borg Star fires, and the Founders' homeworld explodes.

With the Jem'Hadar, the Breen, and the Vorta free from the Founders, their forces turn against the Borg. This time, they fight not for their former Changeling masters but for their own newfound freedom.

It doesn't make a damned bit of difference. The Borg Star systematically obliterates each and every one of the three races' homeworlds and then moves on to secondary targets. It assimilates planets that it can take, but where it finds too much resistance, it simply slaughters the entire globe.

After witnessing the Borg Star tearing through the Dominion's former troops, the _Millennium Falcon_ shoots a message off to both the Galactic Empire and the Rebel Alliance. If the Borg Star comes to their galaxy, they are all doomed.

The Rebellion heroes on the _Falcon_ decide to hunt for help in this galaxy, for some ally against the Borg. They find it in the Alpha Quadrant.

The Federation calls an emergency meeting on Earth and asks the Klingon Empire and the Romulan Star Empire to join them in an alliance against this new Borg/Dominion threat. After confirming the stories of the people aboard the _Falcon,_ the three governments unanimously agree to join forces, hoping that it might somehow be enough.

Captain Jean-Luc Picard points out that the Borg Star's hyperspace drive outclasses even their finest Warp drives. They need ships with hyperdrives now, and they have no time to build them.

Skywalker contacts the Emperor and Mon Mothma to inform them of the growing peril. He asks them to set aside their differences and join together in sending every ship they can spare so that they might have a chance to defeat the Borg Star. They agree, and they both come (along with Vader) to personally lead their forces.

The Imperial and Rebel forces arrive in the Alpha Quadrant just ahead of the Borg Sphere. As the Emperor spies it for the first time, he smiles.

Vader requests a moment alone with Skywalker, who begrudgingly grants it. Vader reveals to Skywalker that he is the young Jedi's father. He proposes that they kill the Emperor, whom Vader is sure will betray them. Shocked by this revelation, Luke storms off and refuses to have anything to do with Vader.

On the evening before the great battle against the Borg Star is to begin, the Emperor and Darth Vader fly out alone to the Borg Star and ask to parley with its leader. A Borg Queen permits them to board, and a platoon of Borg stormtroopers escort them to her throne room. The Borg Queen insists on assimilating the Emperor, which he allows her to do, ordering Vader not to interfere.

When the assimilated Emperor opens his eyes, the Borg Queen screams. Palpatine has taken control of the Collective from her. He is now the Borg Emperor.

To prove to himself that he is the one who controls the Collective, and not the other way around, Palpatine decrees that Vader shall not be assimilated. A large portion of Vader is already cybernetic, after all. However, the Emperor is not so merciful with the rest of the Imperial fleet. Sending Borg stormtroopers over to each of the Imperial starships, he begins their assimilation. These new Borg ships immediately turn their attention toward attacking Earth.

The war against the Federation-Klingon-Romulan-Rebel Alliance, now simply called the Alliance, begins. The Borg Emperor orders the Borg Star and the rest of the Borg fleet of cubes, spheres, and diamonds into the Solar System so that it can attack and destroy Earth, which he believes will shatter the Federation's morale. As the Borg Star enters the system on the far side of the Sun from the Earth, the rest of its fleet advances before it to clear the way. It will take some time for the Borg Star to navigate into the proper position to be able to blow up the Earth, but if nothing can stop its progress, Earth is doomed.

The Force ghost of Obi-Wan Kenobi appears to Luke then and tells him of the fate of the Emperor and Vader. They are the key to this battle, if only Luke can reach them. He apologizes to Luke for not telling him of his father's true identity earlier, and he reveals that Princess Leia is Luke's sister.

In the ready room on the *Enterprise,* Picard holds a war conference of his own. He communicates with Captain Janeway in the *Voyager,* Ambassador Spock in the *Jellyfish,* and Captain Solo and his friends on the *Millennium Falcon.* They formulate a desperate plan and put it into action.

While the *Enterprise* and *Voyager* lead the Alliance ships in holding off the Borg Empire ships, the *Falcon* races through space at top speed, zooming between the Borg starcraft until it reaches the Borg Star. There, Vader senses Luke and Leia's presence on the ship and orders it brought in via tractor beam.

Once the *Millennium Falcon* is aboard the Borg Star, Luke, Leia, Han, and Chewbacca are captured by Borg stormtroopers and brought before the Borg Emperor and Vader. The Emperor orders the lot of them assimilated, but he offers to make an exception for Luke and Leia if they will kill their father for him and become his Dark Apprentices.

Vader starts to battle his children, but he loses his nerve when Leia confronts him. She just looks too much like her mother for him to wish her harm. He turns on the Borg Emperor instead.

As the battle in the throne room rages on, C-3PO and R2-D2 emerge from the *Millennium Falcon* along with Data, who's been remade in the body of B-4. They make their way into the facility and find the shield generator for the sector they're in. They deactivate it, blowing all of the air out of the landing bay and sweeping all of the Borg stormtroopers in the bay out into space.

With the shields down in this one place, Ambassador Spock can do his job. Using a cloaking device that the Romulans fitted into the *Jellyfish* for him, along with a transporter amplifier, he has been sitting outside the Borg Star, waiting for his chance. He enters the bay and begins to prepare the red matter.

Back in the throne room, the Borg Emperor slays Vader with Force lightning. This leaves him open to attack, and Skywalker hurls his lightsaber at Palpatine, slicing him in half at the waist. This only buys Vader a short reprieve, as the Borg Emperor reveals that most of his body below his chest has been replaced with Borg cybernetics.

Vader reels back into his children's arms, and Chewbacca catches him, holding him upright. The Borg Emperor cackles as he prepares to use his Force lightning against all of them at once. Soon they shall be assimilated, and the entire galaxy shall belong to him. And once he triumphs here, his home galaxy will be next.

As the Borg Emperor speaks, the Rebels and Vader are beamed away. They materialize in the *Jellyfish* and find themselves standing next to C-3PO, R2-D2, and Data. Spock says, "Are you ready, Captain?"

"Affirmative," says Picard.

"On my mark," Spock says. He hits a button, and the entire container of red matter is beamed away. "Now!"

The people, droids, and android aboard the *Jellyfish* disappear and reappear in the *Enterprise*'s transporter room. "We've got them!" Geordi La Forge reports to Captain Picard.

On the viewscreen on the bridge, Picard can see a black hole starting to form near the Borg Star's laser dish, consuming the space station. The red matter made it into the center of the Borg Star's reactor core, which activated it. They have only seconds to get away before the black hole sucks them in as well.

Picard barks at his helmsman. "Lieutenant Crusher! Maximum Warp! Engage!"

As Wesley Crusher pilots the *Enterprise* away from the Borg Star at Warp speed, every other ship in the Alliance does the same, leaving the Borg Star and the rest of the ships from the Borg Empire—stunned at the sudden loss of their new Emperor—to be consumed.

RESULT: The good guys win—for now.

Index

DAILY BENDER

Want Some More?

Hit up our humor blog, The Daily Bender, to get your fill of all things funny—be it subversive, odd, offbeat, or just plain mean. The Bender editors are there to get you through the day and on your way to happy hour. Whether we're linking to the latest video that made us laugh or calling out (or bullshit on) whatever's happening, we've got what you need for a good laugh.

If you like our book, you'll love our blog. (And if you hated it, "man up" and tell us why.) Visit The Daily Bender for a shot of humor that'll serve you until the bartender can.

Sign up for our newsletter at

www.adamsmedia.com/blog/humor

and download our Top Ten Maxims No Man Should Live Without.